GW00544986

ASSESSMENT IN PRIMARY AND MIDDLE SCHOOLS

ROUTLEDGE TEACHING 5–13 SERIES
Edited by Colin Richards, formerly of the School of
Education, Leicester University.

Assessment
in Primary and Middle Schools

MARTEN SHIPMAN

ROUTLEDGE

First published 1983 by Croom Helm
Reprinted in paperback 1987
Reprinted 1989 by Routledge

11 New Fetter Lane, London EC4P 4EE
29 West 35th Street, New York, NY 10001

© 1983 M. Shipman

Printed and bound in Great Britain by
Billings & Sons Limited, Worcester

British Library Cataloguing in Publication Data

Shipman, Marten
    Assessment in primary and middle schools.
    1. Grading and marking (Students)
    I. Title
    372.1'2'64   LB3051
    ISBN 0-415-04305-0

Assessment in Primary and Middle Schools is a set book for the MA in
Education Module E811 Educational Evaluation.

CONTENTS

FIGURES

FOREWORD

Teaching 5-13 is a series of books intended to foster the professional development of teachers in primary and middle schools. The series is being published at a time when there are growing demands on teachers to demonstrate increasing levels of professional understanding and competence. Although the importance of personal qualities and social skills in successful teaching is acknowledged, the series is based on the premise that the enhancement of teacher competence and judgement in curricular and organisational matters is the major goal of pre-service and in-service teacher education, and that this enhancement is furthered, not by the provision of recipes to be applied in any context, but by the application of practical principles for the organisation and management of learning and for the planning, implementation and evaluation of curricula. The series aims to help teachers and trainee teachers to think out for themselves ways of tackling the problems which confront them in their own particular range of circumstances. It does this by providing two kinds of books: those which focus on a particular area of the primary or middle school curriculum, and those which discuss general issues germane to any area of the curriculum.

In this book Marten Shipman deals with the vexed question of assessment in primary and middle school education. Since the mid-seventies there has been much talk about assessment and evaluation, much of it esoteric or impractical for those in school to implement. Too often, adopting such suggestions would mean taking time away from teaching rather than informing and developing its practice. Marten Shipman's book is different and, in a sense, unique. It starts from where teachers are and what they do, and suggests how they can develop their everyday judgements into more dependable, defensible ones. In it, teachers are offered a range of possibilities for evaluating children's learning and the school as an organisation. These possibilities can be taken up to varying degrees depending on the individual's circumstances and concerns. It constitutes a much-needed, practical contribution to the issue of assessment at the primary stage.

Colin Richards

INTRODUCTION

This book is about evaluation in primary and middle schools. It starts in the classroom. Teachers judge situations, the attainments of children, their own teaching styles, and adjust their approach on the basis of this impressionistic evaluation. Instead of offering research designs, test constructions and statistical techniques, the book contains suggestions for developing the many everyday snap evaluations into more dependable forms.

In a similar way, the evaluation of the school as an organisation, the subject of the second half of the book, starts with the snap judgements that abound in staffroom and headteacher's study. Ways are suggested of making these more systematic. In common with the chapters on pupils, the aim is to encourage an approach, a model, a perception of evaluation, as an integral part of teaching.

In all aspects of everyday life we are continually deciding on possible courses of action by considering available evidence, however scanty. In teaching, most evaluations have to remain as snap judgements, as there is no time to consult records or diagnose thoroughly when chaos is threatening a classroom or a child is confusing place values. Observing teachers at work suggests that they use a realistic, coherent, if implicit and sometimes casual approach to evaluation as a basis for action. But there are times when impressions are not enough, because the action that follows will have important consequences for children, often beyond the control of the teacher concerned. The conventional textbook on evaluation tends to present techniques which, if adopted, would leave little time over for teaching. Instead, this book aims at ways of improving evaluation to match the importance of the actions that will follow. Most can be left as instantaneous judgements. A few will need organising with care into textbook order. In between, teachers will give priority to evaluation according to the importance of the decisions that have to be made.

Developing models of evaluation for use in the school means that it is seen not only as a part of all teaching, but as merged with professional judgement. Structuring evaluation is useful because it can produce more dependable evidence for the exercise of that judgement. Even the most objective assessment technique produces results that have to be interpreted before action can be taken. Furthermore, the technique itself will have had professional judgements built into its design and scoring. This does not make educational evaluation any less useful than medical testing or the consultation over legal cases in a lawyer's office. Indeed, a doctor or a lawyer who relied solely on a test or on precedent as a guide would be culpable. Evaluation does not replace professional judgement; it is part of the much larger armoury used in making decisions.

The absence of any clear distinction between assessment and evaluation is deliberate, and follows from the judgement built into both. The term assessment, usually taken to mean finding out about attitudes, knowledge or skills, is used when the collection of information is being discussed. Evaluation, usually defined as judging performance, is used when the activity involves interpretation of that performance. But the two are not in reality divisible. To divide them suggests that there is some completely objective approach free of the values of the designer. This seems to me misleading. There are not two distinct poles, one objective, the other subjective, but a spectrum from one to the other. Most teachers have to move easily to and fro along that spectrum, but most of the time are under pressure near the subjective end, using their professional judgement. This may often be arbitrary and expedient, but it seemed more useful to improve the reliability of this practice than to hope for a sudden adoption of assessment techniques on any large scale.

The absence in this book of any clear distinction between assessment and evaluation is only one aspect that will worry the technically minded. But it is the justification for starting with what teachers do rather than with what they should do technically. The model that teachers use works for them because it can be instantaneous and effective. It does not require extended preparation, or technical expertise. Hence it fits the thinking-on-the-feet that is one of the main skills of teaching, particularly in the primary and middle schools. In further and higher education it is possible to teach a course by sticking rigidly to the syllabus, to lecture notes, preparing for an examination that takes the same form year after year. This would be nonsense in the infant classroom, and grossly inflexible for younger children.

Resistance to assessment usually comes from teachers who accept the philosophy of the Plowden Report of 1967, which was itself summarised in the Hadow Report of 1931, defining primary schooling 'in terms of activity and experience rather than of knowledge to be acquired and facts to be stored' (Hadow, 1931, p. 93). However, the emphasis in this book is on professional judgement as the basis of evaluation. This should make it useful to all teachers as long as they accept that they have the responsibility for organising the framework for promoting worthwhile activities among children, and for the effectiveness of the school in which these processes occur.

The same approaches are recommended for the evaluation of the school as an organisation as well as of the attainments of pupils. In the last decade many LEAs have produced documents to help the staff of schools evaluate their work. The schemes introduced range from mandatory to voluntary, through many others where the answers to the questions asked are used on in-service courses, or form the basis of discussions between local advisors or inspectors, and the teachers. But each of these lists of questions contains the prescriptions of those who designed them. The questions are not neutral. They define a version of the well-run school. This applies to all such self-evaluation schemes, whether produced in county or town hall, or academia. Once again we are in the world of evaluation containing professional judgements. Consequently, it seemed most useful to start, as for the evaluation of pupil attainment, with the snap judgements of headteachers and teachers about their schools. These are prescriptive, as are externally produced self-assessment schemes. The book presents ways of making this self-assessment explicit, and in particular of relating it to the way teachers see the organisation of their schools.

Thanks are due to the many teachers who have discussed the proposal for this book, and especially to those who let me observe them in the classroom. Jim Campbell, through advice and from the evidence of his own research on middle schools, kept me informed about recent developments. Colin Richards, as General Editor of the series in which this book belongs, read the typescripts in their crude state and gave invaluable guidance. To these and to many others who encouraged me in this work I am very grateful.

PART ONE

EVALUATING THE PUPILS

1 ASSESSMENT AS A PART OF TEACHING

Here is a selection of the activities of a primary schoolteacher, with a class of ten-year-olds, which I observed during one morning's work.

(1) Explaining to the whole class, and to individual children, why they went wrong in some of their work grouping regular and irregular shapes.
(2) Advising the class and individuals how to avoid similar mistakes from there on.
(3) Commenting on the quality of individual work and giving it a 'Good', 'Fair' or 'Poor' with a red ball-point pen.
(4) Moving children from one group to another to match them to the level of work of the others in the groups.
(5) Talking to me about the probable success or failure of individual children in the years to come.
(6) Discussing with the children as a class, and later with myself, the quality of the work just completed.

These six activities could be found in many primary or middle school classrooms. They are part of normal teaching activities as children are helped to overcome difficulties, encouraged so that they carry on working cheerfully and productively, and given some idea of the quality of work they are doing. It is also normal for teachers to make adjustments to the curriculum as they go, and plan to change the ways things are to be done in the future. Those six activities could be labelled Diagnosis, Guidance, Grading, Selection, Prediction and Evaluation. These are the major purposes of assessment identified by Macintosh and Hale (1976). Teaching and assessment are inseparable.

The impossibility of separating teaching from assessment can be observed wherever teaching occurs. As the teacher spoke to the class, or to individual children, she was helping by judging how well they were doing, how they could do better, and how she could organise the work to help. Much of this assessment was instantaneous and spontaneous. Here we have a brief, lively session on multiplication tables. Within ten minutes there are all six assessment procedures. The teacher assesses through her ability to detect understanding and bewilderment, enthusiasm and boredom, minority and majority understanding. Sometimes it

1

is assessment based on answers given, but it can be through the light in the eyes of the children, the waxing and waning of enthusiasm. As the teacher interprets signs from the children there is an immediate curriculum development, changes in teaching style, emphasis, speed or topic. Discussing this over coffee after ninety minutes on the move, the teacher remarked

> It's never the same, even if I plan it to be. They can be asleep one day and bubbling the next. You have to see how it is going and adjust. You've also got to jolly some along and stop others getting all the attention. I suppose you learn it as you do it.

That teacher did very little formal assessing beyond occasional grading in an impressionistic way, filling in a report card at the end of each year showing progress in the basic skills and a grade for overall attainment, and collecting examples of good work to pass on to the next teacher. Yet her work was full of decisions based on rapid assessments, and over the years it had been continually re-designed as she judged this approach to be better than that. Jackson and Belford (1965), observing American elementary school teachers, concluded that they were continually assessing, and as a consequence were changing teaching styles and curriculum after close attention to the faces of the children. The joy of teaching came through the light in the eyes of the children. That light provided the feedback required for instantaneous re-planning.

It is the merging of teaching and assessing that accounts for the recommendations in this book. Whether the focus is on assessing to help children, or to develop curriculum, or to improve school organisation, it has to be usable by teachers who are already engaged in such activity. It is aimed at making such activity systematic and coherent, and this involves more emphasis on new ways of thinking about assessment than techniques for undertaking it. Whether looking at the way learning is organised or at the effectiveness of the school, at the way children are learning or the way they are graded, the key is seen to be to move forward from what is already going on, not to produce the sophisticated, time-consuming and expensive statistical assessments that appear in most books. It is more productive to present a model for assessment that if adopted would use existing practices, while enabling new ones to be built on to them.

In moving towards a model that can be used to help in teaching and to produce information on the running of schools, it is necessary to ask a number of questions about the purposes of assessment and the use to be made of the information collected. These questions are often met in books through technical terms. These are a shorthand expressing practices that daily. engage every teacher. They deal with very important issues, but in the end are concerned with just those things which occur every day in every classroom. The jargon can be off-putting, which is a pity given the importance of the ideas it incorporates. Even worse, the specialists can use the ideas as if they were divorced from the messy world of the classroom. This enables academics to improve their models, but decreases their relevance to the real world. Thus, the questions that follow are designed to introduce a few technical ideas, but also to ground them in the reality of teachers. There is loss in this pragmatic approach, and in Chapter 4 steps to improve the technical quality of tests are outlined. But the way to more useful assessment, and hence to more effective teaching, is through an approach rather than a technique.

The approach that is recommended in Chapter 2 is to bear in mind models of assessment that are synchronised with the way teaching is usually organised. The emphasis is on seeing assessment as part of teaching, and then adapting both to improve the way learning is organised. The models are ways of thinking about helping children learn through organising teaching systematically, not blueprints for better tests.

Assessment is about decision-making. Teachers organise curriculum and teaching and need information in the search for effectiveness; but they also help children overcome barriers to learning. In both cases assessment is required, but this is never achieved just through the application of a test. It may help to use a diagnostic test such as the Aston Index (Newton and Thomson, 1976) to try to find out why a child is having difficulties in learning to read. But teachers usually use such tests as a convenient way of getting information in a comprehensive way about a child before bringing their professional judgement to bear. The danger of published tests is that they can be used as a substitute for the judgement of a teacher who knows the child well and has seen the problems and the successes over a long period in natural conditions. Tests help the teacher come to a decision, but that decision should come from all the knowledge that the teacher has accumulated. Hence it is the collection, recording and retrieval of the information that is important; but these in turn depend on the model that the teacher has of the relation of assessment and teaching. The 'picture in the mind' of how we are to get into a position to obtain the necessary information in the right form at the right time is more important than the design of instruments, because it facilitates rather than replaces professional judgement. Teachers take responsibility for organising learning; assessment should be the source of information to make this organisation effective. That requires teaching, learning and assessment to be conceived as inseparable in theory as they are in practice.

Process or Product?

It is usual to distinguish between assessing the products of work and assessing the processes through which they are achieved. The interest may be in giving a grade for a completed project after considering the finished item; but the concern may be more with the way it was produced, the way the children set about collecting, organising and interpreting the information. In the first case attention will be paid to the ideas presented, the quality and quantity of the work, its relevance to the subject set and to evidence or originality. In the second the interest will be on how the work was approached, planned, implemented and presented. In one there is terminal assessment; in the other assessment of ongoing procedures. Indeed, processes can be looked at without the exercise being necessarily completed, and this has the advantage of providing feedback while the work in still proceeding.

The temptation is to concentrate on products in assessment because they are tangible and often measurable. It is far more difficult to assess rather than just describe the way things are done; yet the observation of processes often has to take priority over the grading of products if learning is to be improved. The project, the essay, the sums are specific outcomes of methods employed. They may indicate that the methods have been mastered, but the teacher may have to guess at this. Any model of assessment in schools that can help children has to provide information on how work is being tackled and how it can be done more effectively.

The tendency for the assessment of products to take precedence over looking at processes can be illustrated through the way continuous assessment often works out in practice. In theory this should mean that children are assessed as they work, in order that they can be guided through the feedback obtained. But it rarely works out that way: the observation of the teacher, or the test, or the essay tend to occur when a sequence of work has been finished. By the time the results have been given back, the children are on the next piece of work. The idea of continuous assessment is to continuously feed back useful information, but it is usually used to look at products when it is too late to be useful. Black and Dockrell (1980) describe most continuous assessment as a staccato form of terminal assessment. The only genuine continuous assessment is often the running observations by teachers as they move among the children helping and correcting, diagnosing and remedying.

Sometimes the terms 'formative' and 'summative' evaluation are used to distinguish between looking at ways of improving courses and methods as the work goes on, and looking at what has already been learned or taught. Formative evaluation serves to guide teacher or pupils as they are working. Summative evaluation gives a picture of what has been achieved. Once again the choice is between looking at what has passed and looking at what is happening, while it is happening. As with the process-product distinction there is no clear difference between formative and summative evaluation. The same test may sum up a section of work and produce information on how to adapt methods for the next. But in distinguishing process-product and formative-summative evaluations there is an important conclusion. If you assess when a section of work is over, the assessment cannot help learner or teacher to do things better at the time. The chance has gone before the results are known. It is often necessary to produce evidence on what has been achieved. But it is always necessary to feed information back to children as they learn, to adapt teaching methods, and to develop curricula as circumstances change. Formative evaluation is inseparable from teaching.

The emphasis on evaluation as a formative activity built into the organisation of learning avoids associating it with any one approach to education. Assessment is usually approached as an attempt to quantify outputs, to measure the measurable. It is consequently related to a product-orientated, instrumental view of learning. The output is pre-specified, and success or failure is gauged according to whether the targets have been attained. But in primary schooling in particular there is an alternative view of learning which stresses the intrinsic value of activities, the personal growth that occurs, and the role of the children in determining the direction of events. Learning is not programmed in advance, but is open-ended. Assessment cannot be planned to gauge predictable outcomes.

The advantage of a formative evaluation that is organised to supplement professional judgement is that it fits process as well as product emphases, child-centred as well as teacher-centred. But evaluation does incorporate a constraint: the criteria for judgement have to be spelled out in advance, and they have to be made known to others who may use the evaluation. This is a challenge, for it assumes that there is a curriculum, procedures for facilitating learning and activities which are both encouraged and valued. Evaluation rests on assumptions that actions can be valued, and that the criteria for this can be spelled out. Many readers will rightly suspect that the recommendations made in this book assume that many outcomes of schooling should be pre-specified and consequently evaluated. But if something is valued then the conditions for its development should be thought through. Once they are, evaluation is possible, and two benefits accrue. First, the act of thinking through the activity to establish criteria for judging its success is itself a guarantee that the conditions for worthwhile activities have been carefully considered. Secondly, the evaluation should provide information for improving the conditions under which the learning that is valued will occur.

This discussion of where to focus assessment has provided the first base of a usable model. This has to give clues on the way children are learning and the way that learning is organised, as well as being capable of producing information that will sum up what has been achieved. This information can then be useful for helping thildren as well as grading them. But the need to consider processes as well as products applies also to assessments of the curriculum, teaching methods and school organisation. The interest of teachers, headteachers, governors, parents and the LEA are in both what has been done and how it is being done.

What Reference do you Use?

It is not only teaching that is inseparable from assessment; we are assessed as part of everyday life. This is because people want to know that we are competent to do things, or the best person for the job, or improving or deteriorating as we work or play. We are assessed to check that we are fit to enter the Church, qualified for higher education or sufficiently skilled to drive a car. As life has become complicated in the twentieth century this type of assessment has increased to avoid un-necessary damage to other humans or to organisations, or to machines. But even in simple societies there are tests to see whether young men are fit to be warriors or young women ready to become wives.

Here are three examples of different kinds of assessment. An adult takes a driving test consisting of a check on eyesight, knowledge of the Highway Code and a practical test of set, standard exercises on the road. A child brings home her school report which shows that she has come tenth out of a class of thirty. A golfer, after much practice, has his handicap reduced. In the first example driving competence is being assessed against pre-determined standards consisting of seeing a number plate at 40 yards, answering questions on road use, and showing that the driver is not a danger to other road users. The driving test is against content, criteria, standards, objectives. The child has been assessed by comparison with her peers. The golfer has triumphed through an assessment based on his own previous performance.

The technical term for assessing against some pre-determined standard is *criterion-referenced testing*. An alternative term for this is content-referenced. Also used are objective or domain-referenced. All are terms used to describe assessment that refers performance to work covered, to the content or the domain. But that content is determined, if only implicitly, by consideration of objectives. Thus, the assessment is objective-referenced. But the reference is also to criteria of performance, to mastery of some specified standards. The term content-referenced is used here because the more usual criterion-referenced implies a more technical construction than is feasible for most classroom teachers. As you settle into the dentist's chair it is the knowledge that he has met standards of the college of dentistry, not that he was twelfth out of a class of twenty on graduating that relieves anxiety. The knight's ordeals, the apprentice's masterpiece and the driving test were designed to ensure that competence had been demonstrated. Such assessments of children are essential in school, for they show whether they are ready to go on to the next learning because they have mastered its prerequisites.

In teaching it is rare just to want to know that a child has reached a specified level of attainment, or that the school has reached its target of collecting a ton of waste paper a term. Teachers usually want to know by how much a child has exceeded or fallen short of a predetermined level of performance, or how much more than a ton of paper was collected. This is because teachers want information from assessment that will help them to help the child. The teacher's professional skill comes into play through diagnosing the difficulties facing children, and by implementing remedies. Knowing that a certain level of performance has been attained or failed is a start, for it alerts the teacher to the need to extend mastered ideas, or remedy failures to understand. Ideally, there would be diagnostic tests that would do the job of showing what was wrong and suggesting remedies, but there are few of these available. The advantage of criterion-referenced tests is that they can help identify success or failure against specified levels of performance. That is a basis from which the teacher can use her own judgement of the action required to improve the situation, and this is just what happens in the course of most teaching. Whether formally or informally, teachers judge that a child has reached a satisfactory level or fallen short of it. Some diagnosis of the child and of the curriculum is carried out, and this is followed with practice to extend or remedy performance.

The emphasis on criterion-referenced assessment in this book arises from observing how teachers use this approach in the classroom. Assessing by judging the strengths and weaknesses of children against a specified standard, or against mastery of a skill, or against the ability to apply a method of interpreting information seems natural to teachers. Criterion-referenced assessment is an extension of normal procedures; but it is also the basis of the remedial actions at the heart of teaching. Assessment by referring to content, whether it be skills mastered, information remembered or ideas understood, enables teachers to concentrate on individuals or groups requiring different follow-up work because they have reached different levels. In organising this development or remedial work teachers move from considering the standards set to professional judgements about the reasons for failure, and the opportunities opened by success. Criterion-referenced assessment is used intuitively; but assessment that is systematic can provide a more reliable base than can intuition for the judgements that determine action in the classroom.

There is a danger in recommending criterion-referencing. Another term for them is objective-referenced, and the debate over the use of objectives in the study of the curriculum has kept many academics employed and productive for over thirty years. In the 1960s it was frequently recommended that the success of a curriculum should be measured by specifying in advance changes in behaviour that could be measured at the end. Aided by books on how to define objectives and with Bloom's classification of objectives, the attempt was made to evaluate systematically.

The narrow range of skills and learning that could be assessed in this way was soon under criticism. Creative, aesthetic, emotional, diffused and sensitive aspects could not be measured. Furthermore, the attempt to measure spring can diminish its magic. To preserve the direction provided by objectives, while avoiding the straitjacket of taking only pre-specified changes of behaviour into account, later curriculum developers have used objectives in unspecific, qualitative ways as maps or checklists. The signpost is retained, but not the trainlines. Thus Cooper (1976) lists seventeen objectives in the field of geography, history and social science, but defines these by descriptive statements rather than measurable behaviour. Here is the checklist for 'Communicating Information'.

Detailed checklist for the general objective 'Communicating information'

With reference to his findings, the pupil can

talk to another child
talk informally to the teacher
talk to the rest of the class
produce a tape-recorded report
write a simple account
write an evaluative report
write a poem
write imaginatively
draw or paint to express ideas or feelings connected with the topic
make models
draw an accurate graph (bar graph, pie chart, line graph, etc.)
construct a map
take photographs
make a videotape
compose music
make a visual display
make an audio-visual display

THE PUPIL

knows his own strengths and weaknesses in methods of communication
is prepared to improve his skills in methods of communication, particularly those in which he is relatively weak
can choose a method of communication appropriate to the message
can choose a method of communication and form of the message which is appropriate to the intended receiver
Source: Cooper, 1976, p. 45.

Much assessment by teachers and most standardised tests compare the performance of one child against that of other children. Children may be ranked for comparison or given grades or percentages after consideration of how well they have done against other members of the class. Public examinations at O and A-level tend to be assessed in this way. Similar proportions get an A or B, and so on year after year. Any one student's grade is determined by reference to how well the rest have done. The grade does not refer to a level of performance but to the performance of others. Indeed, in a 'good' year the same performance in liable to get a lower grade than in a 'poor' year because the comparison is against peers, not specified standards. This is *norm-referenced assessment.* Because schools take young children and over ten or more years sort them for very different employment, norm-referenced assessment is still used frequently. But it is often of little use in improving teaching.

The difference between norm and criterion-referencing is important, since grades, marks, comments mean nothing until the reference is known. An A that means 'is in the top 20 per cent of her year group for this subject' is different from an A that means 'can multiply one-figure numbers together with over 95 per cent accuracy'. Most classroom assessments tend to be referenced against norms of performance of the class as a whole. Most published tests, whether of verbal ability, reading or mathematics, reference children to the performance of the group on which they were standardised. The most common content-referenced tests are Brownie, Girl Guide, Cub or Scout tests, and the grades of the Royal College of Music examinations. Here reference is made to specified levels of attainment. Some published tests are now criterion-referenced.   Examples   are   the   *Reynell   Developmental Language Scales* (NFER, 1969) and *Yardsticks* (Nelson, 1975).

There is no clear distinction between the two types of test. To establish criteria of performance in advance we fall back on our knowledge of pupils in general. Our expectations refer to norms even when we are trying to establish expected standards. Similarly, we may set a standard at which we will move children to the next piece of work; but if the numbers who can join in that work are limited and a lot reach the standard, we fall back on comparing performances, referring to norms. Assessment often deliberately mixes the two: children are graded against the attainment of a whole class, but are given higher or lower grades for mastering what the teacher sees as very important ideas or skills. Whatever your performance at thematic work you do not score high unless you can present the work neatly and systematically. But the most common situation is for there to be no reference at all, and the child, other teachers, or parents have no way of knowing what the number or grade refers to. It is this unreferenced assessment that can be misleading.

If most assessments have no reference, the most common method of giving them meaning is to refer to previous performance. The school is said to be doing much better than last year on reading. A child is reported as working less well than before. This is *self-referenced assessment*. This self-referencing is most popular in the classroom where the teaching and assessment coincide. 'Well done, that's much better' or 'Now I think you can work a little faster than that' are typical of this running assessment referring the child to previous performance to judge the present and prepare for the future. There is no time to refer to criteria or to norms. Such self-assessment is also used in reporting formally. The comments in school records or to parents often refer to 'keeping up the good work', to 'room for improvement' or 'pleased with the progress made since last term'. Even where a comparison is made with the rest of the class or year group, or to some national sample on which the standardised test scores are based, or to some specified level of attainment, there is often another grade given for effort, and here it is liable to be a reference to previous work-levels as well as to the norms of peers.

The tendency to mix the various types of reference while assessing arises from the need for teachers to balance different purposes. There is no point in a level of objectivity which destroys the confidence of the child or gives the parent no reason to help improve the situation. It is dangerous to conceal from parents that there is a genuine weakness through exclusively stressing how hard the child works or even how much she has improved. Sometimes you need to refer to levels of performance on selected content, sometimes to attainment compared with that of other children and sometimes to improvements or deteriorations. Teachers refer to criteria, standards, content, to the norms set by other children or to previous personal performance according to the purpose which the assessment is to serve.

Once again, these three forms of referencing can be found in every classroom. Assessment is built into teaching, and the references are varied in the effort to get results. 'I want everybody to be able to do this by the end of the morning.' The criterion level is set and the teacher concentrates on checking that the class have attained it. 'There's no reason why John should be able to do it that well and not you'. The norm is established, and the children are checked to see that they measure up to the Stakhanov or the beaver of the top juniors. 'You're going backwards; it was neater last week.' The past performance is set up as reference, and the teacher compares the new work with it as the child is assessed against her own past. The advantage of defining and labelling the three types of references is that they can then be developed and used more effectively. We all speak prose, knowing that we do has enabled prose styles to be improved.

The obvious objection to building on to the often intuitive and implicit assessment procedures of teachers is that it is liable to produce little that is both credible and objective. This is a danger, and there would be no point in merely recommending techniques that compounded errors or bias. But it has already been argued that the model is basically sound, and coincides with that recommended for the diagnostic assessment of pupils. Similarly, it is suitable for evaluating the school as an organisation. The techniques recommended are designed to increase the weight that can be placed on the evidence collected. The tests applied to any kind of evidence have to be applied here, and I have posed these as four related questions.

How Reliable was the Assessment?

A detective asks, 'Can I depend on this evidence?' He can if his methods of collecting the evidence would always yield similar results. Litmus paper is a reliable indicator of acidity. Every assessment should be accompanied by this question about reliability, which concerns the methods and the chances that they might account for very different results every time they were used. Without reliable techniques to assess or guide judgement there is only guesswork about the value of the evidence.

How Valid is the Evidence?

The second question should be directed at the evidence rather than the means through which it was collected. Is it really a close approximation to the truth, an appropriate indicator of the aspect under consideration? Are those test results really a full measure of reading, or that level of right answers an indicator of mastery of aesthetic appreciation? Very often the only way of checking validity is by collecting together judgements from different people. However crude, such checks ensure that one person's opinion is not accepted as necessarily true.

These are two basic questions, and they will be asked as techniques are recommended and the nature of acceptable evidence discussed. But evidence from assessment is often used as a basis of generalisation; and this can be from one child to many, from this group to the whole class, from this week's work to the whole year, from that estate to the whole environment of the school and so on, necessitating a third question.

How Far Can You Generalise from the Evidence?

Over-generalisation is very common; we jump from the individual to the general case with ease. Methods of training American pigeons to work for their food are recommended for English primary school children, and guidance for neurotic Viennese used as a basis for pastoral care in middle schools. It is questionable whether those results for Jane's religious education one week are a guide to her consistent performance in the subject, and certainly not of her general state of grace. This is a particular problem when reporting consistent performance of the school. Few indicators are available and these are used elastically. Two road-safety certificates do not make a caring school, nor the county prize for the best poem an academic community. Very often the reader of a report or record has to take this and the question about reliability and validity on trust. There is not sufficient information to enable the answers to be given even if the questions are asked. Thus, there is a fourth question.

Is There Sufficient Information to Enable the Basic Questions to be Answered?

Information from assessment is valuable to other teachers, to parents, to the pupils, to governors or the LEA, only if it can be interpreted. They have to know what that grade means and what was the basis for that comment. Is that B to be referred to some scatter of grades across the class? Or to the year group, or to children of that age as a whole? Is it for attainment or effort or some mix of both? Does 'The school continues to maintain a high standard of written work' mean that there has been a comparison with other schools or against some national indicator provided by the Assessment of Performance Unit (APU)? Or is it a professional judgement or wishful thinking? What is the child to do when faced with the comment 'This is not up to your usual standard' on his topic work, when he has no idea where he has slipped from grace? Evidence from assessment has to be referred to some criteria, norm or performance, and the basis has to be made clear to the audience if it is to be useful.

2 IMPROVING THE QUALITY OF EVALUATION

In this chapter steps are outlined to add reliability and validity to the everyday impressionistic evaluations of teachers as they go about their work. The intention is to present a way of improving the quality of the small part of the total evaluating of teachers that they select as too important to remain as snap judgements. The steps can be taken as far as is feasible given the time and energy available, but any step is likely to improve the quality. Furthermore, the first steps are easy to take, and promise the largest benefits for the least effort.

Most evaluation in the classroom will remain instantaneous and impressionistic. It is needed to motivate, direct and re-direct, check, encourage and reward. At the other extreme a very small sample of the work of children will be selected for thorough assessment because it is to be reported to parents, or used to group, or to transfer to different schools or to pass to other teachers. In between working procedures and formal reporting, a lot of evaluation will feed back information to children, will inform the teacher, ensure that work is going ahead smoothly. This information is used for monitoring and maintenance. It is not used for making critical decisions, but needs to be more than working impressions. By starting with the teacher in the classroom and progressively organising impressionistic evaluations, choice is left with the teacher on how far to move to provide an appropriate response to the need for information. Instead of an all-or-nothing choice, there is a range of possibilities.

The sequence recommended is in three parts. The first step is to see evaluation within the organisation of learning as recommended in Chapter 1. The second step is to clarify the purposes of the evaluation, the methods to be used and the use to be made of the results. The third step is progressively to structure the evaluation. This sequence follows from the approach outlined in Chapter 1. If evaluation is to be a part of teaching, then first it has to be seen that way; secondly, seen as having specific uses; and thirdly, as technically feasible.

Step 1: Seeing Evaluation Within the Organisation of Learning

Here we are at the heart of the approach to evaluation that is recommended in the chapters that follow. It would be pretentious to call it diagnostic, so the term 'formative' is used. But by following the sequence used by teachers as they go about their job, an approach can be traced out that not only fits that used in practice, but more importantly, draws on the skills used by teachers as they organise learning. Evaluation is geared to helping children learn. This formative approach has been furthest developed by the Scottish Council for Educational Research (SCRE, 1977), and the model used here owes most to that work.

Figure 2.1: Conventional Continuous Assessment

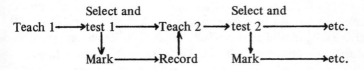

Figure 2.2: Assessment as Part of the Organisation of Learning

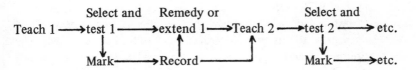

A look at Figure 2.1 shows how most assessment that is planned has little chance of benefiting children. It comes at the end of a piece of work and even at the end of a term or year. Black and Dockrell (1980, pp. 25-30) have pointed out that even continuous assessment suffers from this bad timing. It is rarely continuous in providing running feed-back to children, but merely phased at more frequent intervals than conventional tests or examinations. It is, in Black's term, 'staccato' rather than continuous assessment. As such it is as terminal as the end-of-term examination, and as little use for providing information that could help teacher or learner.

Thinking about evaluation with Figure 2.2 in mind is the first step in improving its usefulness. In Scotland the attempts to produce a genuinely diagnostic assessment of this kind in even a few areas of a few subjects have proved very time-consuming. But it is the model that matters. Of course, the effort soon comes up against the subject of most books on assessment: the design of reliable and valid tests. But a lot can be done before much effort is exerted on technical-design issues. This involves starting with Figure 2.2 in mind, and then building into the working assessments of teachers the controls that will make them more useful when hundreds of decisions that affect each child every term are being made.

The switch to a formative model brings evaluation into the organisation of learning, where it belongs. Some assessment of outcomes is necessary for grading, selection and prediction. Here the priority is to get reliable and valid assessments. Chapters 3 and 4 provide help in the construction and the use of tests, but the majority of evaluations are for the diagnosis, the guidance and the immediate feedback that are the stock-in-trade of teachers. These everyday activities rest on formative evaluation. Whether instantaneous and impressionistic, or carefully constructed and validated, formative evaluation provides the information that can be used to guide teaching.

Ideally, evaluation should be fully diagnostic, providing teachers with information on why children fail or succeed, but such diagnostic techniques are time-consuming to construct. It is also often beyond our existing knowledge to uncover the reasons why children perform as they do. A formative approach to evaluation can be more superficial, yet still useful. It need not provide reasons or causes of failure or success, but it can alert teachers to strengths and weaknesses, and enable teachers to bring their professional judgement to bear. The evaluation guides and supplements the teachers' judgement; it does not replace it. A mother might not know what is wrong with a fretful, feverish child, but can still take precautions on detecting the high temperature. Psychologists and sociologists cannot provide teachers with diagnostic tools to detect all specific learning difficulties, but knowing that these exist enables the teacher to help the child. Causes of problems are elusive, but help is still possible. That is the reason why Figure 2.2 is useful: it is aligned to professional practice.

The switch in the perception of assessment from summative at the end of a section of work, to formative to help the children learn is an important first step in increasing the value of assessment. The formative model is built on the practice of most teachers. The advantages of making it the explicit basis of assessment accrue to both pupils and the teacher. Thinking through sequences of work with formative evaluation in mind, ensures that the chance of some children missing out is reduced. In this sense evaluation is a step towards being fair to the children who have difficulties; but it is also a way of ensuring that teachers obtain information on the effectiveness of the way they are organising learning. This use of evaluation as an integral part of planning is a feature of most teaching. Having the explicit formative model in mind is a start to useful assessment.

Here we come to the take-off point for discussing evaluation in detail. It should not be a technical exercise imposed after a course is in operation. As any teacher who looks for a standardised test for reading or mathematics realises, the validity is often low because the test does not match the content. LEA or national test programmes are useful in providing rough indicators of standards, but in schools assessment should arise from the planning of work. As the important aspects of learning are decided, so is their assessment. This not only increases the chances of validity because it is built into the planning of the work, but settles its place in the sequence of learning. Assessment is built in, whether implicitly or explicitly, whether impressionistic or systematic, whether instantaneous or planned. It is part of the organisation of learning.

The most important consequence of this placing of assessment in the learning process is to shorten the time between learning and the feedback of information about performance. Most assessment is terminal, and takes place so long after the learning that it cannot provide information to help teacher or child on the next step, nor motivate either. As an example let us take the learning of modern languages. While most of this occurs in secondary schools, the lesson of recent developments is important for younger children.

Dissatisfaction with public examinations that took place at the end of schooling for the majority, led teachers to look at the early years of language teaching. Working parties of teachers in many local authorities have developed graded objectives in modern languages, assessed by graded tests. In Oxfordshire, for example, speaking, listening and reading in a sample of foreign languages are tested using teacher-made materials. The tests are geared to the content of the courses, and there are different levels so that beginners can soon see results from their efforts and teachers get feedback. There is no wait until pupils reach 16 years to obtain the motivation of success. The tests closely reflect the content of the course, and can be taken by individual pupils as they are ready, rather than being imposed on a selected sample as a group. Above all they are graded, cumulative steps to learning a language. The objectives in speaking, listening and reading determine the content of the tests, and they are designed not to differentiate between pupils, but to indicate whether an individual has achieved a specified level of attainment. The certificates provide tangible evidence of success during the course, not just as it finishes (Harrison, 1982).

These graded tests in modern-language teaching can be seen as an example of the principle that the assessment that is likely to be used is that derived from a teaching model for assessment. Teachers of modern languages, as for any subject, assess off-the-cuff in their classrooms to provide instantaneous indications of success, to obtain feedback on how they are doing, to diagnose, shift direction, re-organise content. Discontented with the state of modern-language teaching, particularly for the less able, and in particular seeing the waste of information in public examinations once the course is over, teachers moved to graded objectives and tests. Similarly, this book follows the same procedures. Evaluation is a state of mind, a model, not a series of techniques. It is always present as teachers do their work. Most of it can be left as an instantaneous working technique. But that small part that is used to make important decisions about children or about the curriculum, needs to be thought about more carefully.

Step 2: Clarifying the Approach to Evaluation

Once evaluation is seen as a state of mind, a model, rather than a technique, its place in the organisation of learning is clear. But it is also necessary to be clear about the way evaluation is to be organised before starting on it. Evaluation is time-consuming, and a few questions before starting can save a lot of wasted effort later. These questions refer to the purposes which the evaluation will serve, the methods that will be used for collecting information, and the way it will be fed into the organisation of learning.

Purpose

Why choose this aspect for evaluation?

The recommendation here is for some rapid cost-benefit analysis. Asking why it is worth evaluating here rather than there ensures that you are clear about the purposes of the exercise. In Chapter 1 six uses of evaluation were listed, each of which could be used to take important decisions about children. They could also be used to prepare an account of activities in the classroom. Again, they could be used to help prepare work for the future. In many cases teachers are asked to produce evaluations for headteacher or LEA; but only when it is known why the information is being requested can the teacher determine the priority to be given to it.

Definition

What is going to be assessed?

Very frequently evaluations are global. The child is good, fair or poor, but it is not made clear in what. Definition in advance does not require anything sophisticated; it means distinguishing between assessment of attainment, or effort, or ability or improvement or deterioration, or promise, or behaviour. The grade or comment should not be a halo signifying some aura of general goodness, nor an unspecified stigma. The definition of what is being assessed adds meaning to the exercise. Furthermore, it takes little time or effort to spell out what is under consideration.

Method

How can my own judgement be controlled through the methods I choose?

Most of this chapter is about ways of improving assessment techniques. But it is useful to consider how impressions can be controlled in advance. A useful model to bear in mind is legal. A jury finally evaluates the case, but the judge ensures that the established procedures are followed, and the jury knows what constitutes evidence and what is necessary to distinguish innocence and guilt. Help is given so that judgement can be controlled. It is a valuable question for the entire spectrum of evaluation used by teachers, from snap judgements to producing transfer data. It can lead to caution, second thoughts, sleeping on it, getting a second opinion from another teacher or comparing evaluations from different techniques. It can lead to following the progressive structuring recommended in the rest of this chapter. Here we are acknowledging the need for controls over judgement and all the personal and professional beliefs that can affect it.

Feedback

How is the information from evaluation to be used to improve learning?

Thinking this through in advance can save a lot of effort. Throughout this book it is stressed that there is no point in organising the time-consuming collection of data that is to be stored away and not used. Evaluation is too important to be wasted. But working out how evaluation is to be used not only saves unnecessary work, it indicates how evaluation should proceed. If it is to motivate then it can remain impressionistic. If it is to inform parents, it needs to be worked on. Sorting information and making it public can be politically sensitive. A few initial thoughts can avoid problems later.

Step 3: Improving Reliability and Validity

With a model of evaluation as part of the organisation of learning and a clear idea of why it is needed and of how it will be used, we can move on to ways of structuring impressions and snap judgements to make them more dependable as bases for action.

At each recommended stage the evaluation is organised further in order to improve validity and reliability. The advantage of such an approach is not merely that teachers can start where they are; it is that they can go as far as their own teaching style, or the policy of the staff of the school, determine. Any step taken is likely to improve the quality of assessment and the first steps are easy to take. How many steps are taken will depend on the importance attached to producing dependable information on the performance of children.

Stage 1: Selection of Key Aspects

Practice	*Structure by:*	*To produce:*
Running,	Selecting key aspects	Checkpoints
impressionistic	for evaluation	Guidelines
evaluations.		Lists of basic skills

While running evaluations are a part of the armoury of teachers in keeping learning in the classroom going, there are decisions about children that require the investment of time and effort in evaluating. Where information is to be given to parents or other teachers or other schools, it needs more than a cursory mark out of ten or an instantaneous comment. Secondly, there are some aspects of learning that are so important that missing them is a serious handicap. Here too evaluation has to be thorough to ensure that the basis for further learning has been mastered.

Teachers usually recognise the need to be careful when having to discriminate between children on the basis of ability or attainment. This is where most standardised tests are used. In the basic skills such as reading, writing, listening or arithmetic, it is also recognised that some steps are essential for later learning. Multiplication tables are an obvious example; until they are mastered children are given regular and evaluated practice. But there are many such key points, not only within conventional subjects, but in the study skills that span all of them. Stephens (1977) calls these 'checkpoints', and likens the passage through them to the compulsory points of call in a car rally. It is not necessary to check progress on every part of the course, but there have to be sufficient checkpoints to ensure that nobody is being left too far behind to have any chance of keeping-up or catching-up.

While guidelines for mathematics and language are the most frequently produced by LEAs, teachers are advised about the content of most areas of the curriculum through the selection and definition of key areas. Here, for example, is a section from the *ILEA Music Guidelines* (ILEA, undated) dealing with assessment and evaluation. Each set of questions under the sub-titles 'Assessment and Evaluation in the Classroom: Attitudes, Listening, Performing, Inventing'; 'The Teachers: Organisation, Content, Response and School Reports' defines the subject content by a series of questions.

Listening
1. Are the pupils aurally alert? Do they recognise and respond to sounds only when directed, or on their own initiative?
2. Can they memorise and identify sounds previously heard? Does aural memory have a limited span of short examples or does their memory accurately retain lengthy examples over a long period?
3. Do they recognise aural patterns (repetitions)?
4. Can they recognise differences of pitch, intensity, timbre, rhythm and duration? Is this recognition of broad differences or minute changes?
5. Can they recognise differences of style and period? Are they aware of musical and social influences upon the examples to which they are listening?

The selection of even a few checkpoints for assessment gives the teacher a basis for important decisions about children and about the work that needs doing next. It can also provide feedback to children on the important points selected for assessment. But selection is also necessary for checking the development of attainments that are not as easily listed or tested as basic skills and concepts. Yet teachers do, for example, assess whether children have developed a sense of responsibility, self-criticism, or the ability to express thoughts clearly. These qualities are once again selected out because they are deemed important. They are often found on record cards or reports and are the subject of discussions with pupils and parents.

The procedure for assessing complicated behaviour-patterns remains selection followed by definition. Here, for example, are three examples from the 53-item checklist produced by Harlen (1977), working with teachers to structure observation in order to match activities to children's development of scientific concepts and attitudes. These checklists and the record based on them were designed as guides to what to look for in the behaviour of children and as a framework for keeping records on progress of individuals and the class. Full information on their use can be found in *Match and Mismatch: Raising Questions* (Harlen, 1977).

APPLYING LEARNING

Rarely makes use of previous learning in a new situation without help or guidance	Makes an attempt at tackling new problems but may fail through applying skills or knowledge which are not relevant	Generally uses relevant previous learning to help with new problems

CAUSE AND EFFECT

Accepts that things happen and mechanical things work without seeking for a cause, or suggests reasons in terms of fantasy or mystery	Gives explanations in terms of the presence of some component or feature which may play some part in the process but is not itself the cause. Has difficulty predicting what he thinks may happen when certain changes are made	Seeks to explain physical effect in terms of physical causes even though the correct causal relationship may not be found. Uses the cause-effect relationship observed to suggest what will be the result of certain changes

CLASSIFICATIONS

When he groups objects together there is no consistency between the objects in the groups and his declared intentions in grouping	Can consistently separate things which have a chosen feature from those which do not but cannot then select a different feature and regroup the objects according to that feature	Having sorted objects into groups according to one feature can re-sort the same things according to a different feature which he selects himself

Source: Harlen, 1977, p. 254.

These examples were produced for the 8 to 13 age-range. The inventory of attitudes produced by Harlen is sophisticated and would be time-consuming to use. Elliott (1982) has evaluated it as not being accepted as practicable by teachers. But many teachers use similar home-made definitions of qualities they see as important. This is most common in the early years of schooling. A report on a child in the first school will often consist of a general comment followed by a few sentences on language, number, expressive and creative work, physical development and so on. There may be some finer division of the content such as reading, writing, listening and speaking, under the title 'Language'. This elementary specification of content ensures that users of the assessment know what is being assessed, and appreciate the priorities of teachers. Here is a section from a typical 'Language' checklist designed to ensure that children master selected basic skills.

Speech	Always	Sometimes	Never
Speaks clearly			
Can tell a story —			
to whole class			
to teacher			
Can understand direction given			
Can give directions to other children			
Can answer the telephone			
Can pass on a telephoned message			
Etc.			

This selection of key aspects is a development of normal teaching procedure. It can avoid the discontinuity that can penalise children through failure of important early stages of work. It can provide information for teachers taking over a new class or receiving a new pupil into an established class. But it can be misleading, particularly if used for reporting on children to other teachers or to parents. They don't know what 'always', 'sometimes' or 'never' mean, because they don't know the standards being applied. They require norms or criteria or some level of previous performance against which the evaluation received can be interpreted.

Stage 2: Referencing to Criteria (or Content), Norms or Earlier Performance

Practice	*Structure by:*	*To produce:*
Selected checkpoints	Referencing to	(a) Checklists, profiles,
transfer information	(a) criteria or content	inventories
basic skills	(b) norms	(b) Teacher-made tests
		and grades. Standardised tests
	(c) earlier performance	dardised tests
		(c) Baseline data and
		time series

At this stage the aspects selected by the teacher because of their importance in the learning of pupils, are organised into instruments that can be used and re-used because they have been carefully designed. The selection in the preceding stage will cut down the amount of work that has to be done, but from this point on assessment is more time-consuming because it is likely to be passed to other teachers or to parents or to other schools. Reliability and validity become important because decisions are likely to be made as a result of the assessment, and injustice could result.

The B grade or mark out of 10 or percentage, or 'Good', 'Fair' or 'Bad', or short comment, are often given without any further reference. This makes it impossible to interpret what they mean. Here is an example from the annual report of one of my own children. The grade given was B and the attached comment for the subject read 'It has been a good year'. Now that is comforting to a worried parent. But does the B mean that he is above average, assuming that is denoted by C? Or are most of the class in the B category? But why assume that it is a B in relation to the class rather than the whole year-group? Furthermore, the range might be A to E with similar numbers in each, or A to C in which case it does not look so good. There is also little help when we turn to the comment. Does it mean that he has learned a lot, fulfilled promise, shown ability, worked hard, improved on last year? If it is any of these things, were they in comparison to the rest of the class, or assessed against some absolute standard? In practice the grade and comment yield no information that could lead to action to help, and serve only to give a vague sense that things are going smoothly – so not to worry.

In the three sections that follow assessment is being given a precise meaning by relating it to specified content or relative performance. This is the ground covered by most books on assessment, and recommendations for further reading can be found in Appendix A. Chapter 3 covers the design of tests. Here the focus remains on the model. Here the principle remains that even a little progress towards systematic assessment is worthwhile, so the suggestions made are elementary only. Frequently, however, a greater investment will pay off because well designed content-referenced tests, or well designed teacher-made tests and standardised marks, or carefully chosen standardised tests purchased because they match the curriculum, can be used repeatedly over the years. Once a baseline is defined for a child, improvement or deterioration can be gauged over the years by reference to it.

Criterion or Content-referencing The characteristics of criterion-referenced tests have been described in Chapter 1. They are most useful in assessing whether specified standards or criteria have been achieved. Here the term content-referenced is used because the concern, while still with mastery of skills or knowledge, or concepts, is with aspects of the curriculum that have been learned with, or without, the pre-specification of standards.

Here we are interested in particular material that children have mastered or failed to master. The selection of that material in Stage 1 would have been made after the consideration of objectives. Only the important would be assessed. In this further stage these objectives have to be made the explicit basis of the assessment.

There has been a history of dispute over the use of objectives. This arose through the specification of behavioural objectives that described what pupils should have been able to do after a course of instruction. The objections to this approach were the result of defining the objectives in specific, measurable terms; and this had obvious limitations in the education of younger children in particular, because much of the learning could not be specified in advance. Indeed, the attempt to pre-specify would have destroyed the value of much that is best in contemporary primary and middle school practice. It would be absurd to draw up a list of objectives for the appreciation of beauty or the consideration of the character of Abraham Lincoln.

However, the rejection of curriculum objectives threw the baby out with the bath water. It is just as absurd to suggest that teachers have no objectives in view when they plan their work, as to close options in advance by stating expected outcomes in measurable terms. Objectives are guides to teaching, and are also guides to assessment when mastery of content is being considered. This is the view taken by Blyth *et al.* (1976) in the Schools Council project *Place, Time and Society: Curriculum Planning in History, Geography and Social Science*. This project had the experience of earlier work to draw on, and uses objectives midway between broad aims and narrowly defined behavioural outputs. They are seen as maps for choosing curricula, as they are for starting assessment.

This use of objectives as guides enables assessment to match the breadth of learning in school. Obviously there is loss once the objectives are not defined in terms that enable increments in learning to be measured. But the relaxation enables teachers to stick to the aspects they have selected as important. To illustrate this, here is the framework for evaluation used by the *Place, Time and Society* 8–13 project for the first five of seventeen objectives.

Checklist for assessment over the complete range of the Project's objectives – 1

1 Finding information
   a uses contents page and index
   b looks for more than one source
   c looks for different kinds of source
   d checks one source against another
   e can find sources available inside the school
   f knows where to find appropriate sources outside the school

2 Developing empathy

3 Developing interests

4 Communicating information
   a is able to tell another child about his work
   b writes a clear account of his findings
   c can draw a simple map
   d tries other methods to communicate findings (e.g. poems, music, pictures)
   e varies his communications according to the projected audience

5 Interpreting information
   a can use an atlas independently
   b understands the symbols and conventions of O.S. maps
   c usually understands simple graphs
   d is usually accurate in interpretation of place or period of pictures or photographs

Source: Cooper, 1976, p. 42.

There are many guides for writing objectives (see, for example, Thorndike and Hagen, 1969). When using a relaxed approach they reduce to guidance to ensure maximum clarity, precision and practicality. *Step 1.* State the objectives in terms of behaviour, what the pupil will be able to do, be capable of understanding, or know. Express these as statements that can be ticked to indicate mastery or graded to indicate the level of mastery. *Step 2.* State the objectives in precise terms and focus them on objectives that pre-specify the behaviour expected. Use instructions that use verbs such as define, list, classify, recognise, compare, estimate, predict, generalise, because they were active and focused on behaviour that could be observed or measured. Verbs such as appreciate, understand and feel are too vague. However, if objectives are to be used as guides, such prescriptions would eliminate much of the important work done in primary and middle schools in increasing the understanding, the sense of wonder, the appreciation of beauty and so on. Statements of an objective should be as precise as possible as descriptions of the behaviour expected, but should not be limited to the objectively measurable. Teachers should use their professional judgement over objectives that are only assessable subjectively.

Obviously a classroom teacher will rarely be able to produce anything very sophisticated. But if aesthetic appreciation of creativity or written expression are important objectives, then even a single statement can serve to pass on or pass back to the child some important information than can promote further appreciation. Typical statements by teachers in these areas follow.

'Can give an account of a poem in his or her own words'
'Makes only a limited response and lacks originality'
'Writes technically correct English but lacks flair'

This simple content-referencing can be produced by agreement among groups of teachers and reduces the idiosyncrasy in the judgement. Here, for example, is a list of statements produced by a working party for the Scottish Council for Research in Education (1977) in the aesthetics area.

1. He has a natural and spontaneous response to material the teacher considers aesthetically valuable. He will consistently display a sensitive awareness of form and language. He will take delight in seeking out worthwhile material such as novels, poetry, plays, films, television and so on.
2. He can assimilate complex written material, but needs a little assistance from the teacher. He has a limited understanding of imagery and abstractions in his reading.
3. He usually understands straightforward written material with minimal assistance. He rapidly assimilates simpler material, but is slow to assimilate more complex reading and usually requires the teacher's help for this.
4. He can interpret simple material with the teacher's help. He very rarely understands complex material.
5. He is rarely able to understand any but the very simplest written material.

(pp. 155-6)

Here the numbers 1 to 5 are referenced to a statement, and hence acquire meaning in relation to content. The working out of objectives, even in areas where precision is impossible, is still worthwhile. It can help the teacher clarify aims. It can yield information for better planning next time. It can give the child some idea of strengths and weaknesses. It can inform other teachers or parents of where help will be useful, or where there is a firm base for extending experience. Many statements would be needed to define even part of a complex experience such as aesthetic appreciation, but the effort at providing statements of objectives, however few, is a useful first step.

Once a number of objectives are defined by means of statements there is a checklist ready for use. This samples important aspects of work so that a record of attainment can be built up on children. Either the statements can be graduated as in the Scottish example to give an idea of the level mastered, or single statements can be used with A to E or some other grade, with definitions of each grade to give some idea of the level of mastery.

A checklist is an *aide-mémoire*, enabling the teacher to tick off achievements for the class or for individual pupils. It is a written-down version of the teacher's often implicit planning. Used for individual pupils it tracks them through stages of learning so that the chance of missing important steps is reduced. It will consist of lists of skills to be learned, demonstrated, extended or subject to generalisation.

Once a checklist is designed to cover a range of related attainments, or to identify the various aspects that make up a complicated area of the curriculum such as language or mathematics or history, it becomes an inventory or profile. These are ways of recording progress after consideration of the breadth of the aspect under focus. An inventory can be a stocktaking of the range of pupil attainments. It is selective, but that selection is in the hands of the teacher. Similarly, it is useful to report on a subject such as mathematics using a number of sub-categories.

Checklists, inventories and profiles are content-referenced. They are used by all teachers because they can sample content while supporting regular classroom practice. Their weakness is that there is no standard procedure that secures objectivity, either in the construction of the instrument or in the way grades are given. In practice the principles of construction are the same as those for teacher-made tests and these are discussed in Chapter 3. Clear definition of the quality concerned remains the basis of all checklists, inventories and profiles.

Finally, the alternative names for content-referenced assessment provide an *aide-mémoire* for moving in this direction. Criterion-referencing suggests the need to spell out the standards expected. 'Objective-referenced' suggests the need to be clear of what to look for in the pupil. 'Domain-referenced' suggests the need to sample the area of work that is being assessed. All point towards the overriding purpose of this exercise: to accumulate information on the extent to which pupils have been successful in achieving the goals set by their teachers.

Norm-referencing. Here we are interested in comparing the performance of one child with that of others. This may seem distasteful, but it is an everyday occurrence in schools. Children enter at five, and eleven years later start to enter employment or higher education. On arrival they may seem to be starting from scratch, but on leaving they are sorted into occupations with very different prospects. Teachers sort children out as they encourage them to develop as individuals.

The start of norm-referenced assessment is usually a continuation of the selection of important aspects of learning in Stage 1. The aim is to differentiate between pupils by looking at their attainment, not only of knowledge, but of the skills of acquiring it. To sort pupils out, tests need to yield a broad spread of results. Where the focus is on objectives for content-referenced assessment there need only be a narrow spread as it is mastery of content, not relative position, that matters. In norm-referenced assessment the bright are given scope to outstrip the average, and they in turn to outstrip the dull. Norm-referenced tests are designed to spread children out, not to identify those who have mastered the content.

Most teacher-made and published standardised tests are norm-referenced. This is another indication of the way differentiation is built into everyday teaching. It seems natural to teachers to set a test that will give plenty of opportunities for the bright to be stretched, yet to allow the dull to do something. The aim is rarely to check whether 70 or 80 per cent have mastered the content. The technical design of teacher-made tests is dealt with in Chapter 3 and standardised tests are discussed in Chapter 4. Here the principle of norm-referencing is illustrated through the common practice of grading and the standardisation of marks from tests. In both cases the concern is with reliable comparison.

Rating, or grading, is a tool used by all teachers. Teachers give an A to E without a second thought even to passing phenomena. But without further control such grading is liable to be misleading. It is common to lump grades around the average and not to use extremes. Many teachers mark above the average and are shy of using the lower part of the scale. But the main problem is that there is usually no way of telling what is the average, or the range. Without this detail there is no way of telling whether there is any consistency in the assessments of any one teacher, or in those produced by different teachers. Children may be receiving information about themselves in relation to others that is inconsistent and misleading. Yet important decisions may be made on such assessment. Choices are made between subjects, between streams and groups, between examinations to be taken, prizes to be won, failures to be appreciated, and a thousand clues to whether a child is at the top or bottom, or in the middle of the pile. Some consistency can be introduced by careful design before use or by standardising marks or grades afterwards.

In practice, the everyday marking out of ten that is the commonplace of teaching is usually a mixture of content and norm-referencing. Sometimes there is a deliberate 'marking on the curve'. Here a bell-shaped distribution is assumed, and marks are spread out to give a few at top and bottom with the bulk in the middle. The most elementary rating scales use this normal or some other distribution to help the teacher to compare one child's performance against the rest. Here, for example, are ways in which ratings could be made of a craft such as pottery:

(1) Top 10%:   Top 20%:   Top 40%:   40–60%:   Lower 40%:
(2) Top 25%:   Middle 50%: Lowest 25%:
(3) Among the best quarter:
     Average:
     In the lowest quarter:

There are numerous permutations on this idea that can be used for fine or crude rating. It can be made finer still by stretching the ratings out on a graphical scale as follows. Ticks can then be put at the appropriate place between the 10% marks.

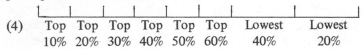

(4) Top   Top   Top   Top   Top   Top   Lowest   Lowest
     10%   20%   30%   40%   50%   60%   40%   20%

Another way of rating is to spell out the comparisons in words. Thus, it is common to use this kind of rough-and-ready way of rating attainment on the subjects.

Subject	Well above average	Above average	Average	Below average	Well below average
Music					
Religious Education					
etc.					

Obviously this type of norm-referenced rating can be combined with content-referenced assessments. Thus, statements reflecting broad objectives can be rated by ranking as above. Technically rating scales are improved until the questions asked or statements ticked or graded give a genuine scale so that there is as much difference between scores of say 10 and 20 as there is between 65 and 75, but these are difficult to construct. Those interested should consult Open University (1982a, Block 4). Conveniently produced rating scales can be improved by the procedures outlined for content-referenced checklists and inventories. Clear, unambiguous definition and a focus of observable performances are once again the basic steps.

Obtaining Consistent Marking After the Assessment. Most of this book builds on the existing practices of teachers. But a line has to be drawn over the release of unstandardised marks to parents, pupils, other teachers or in any public form. These marks are norm-referenced. They compare the performances of children. They are used to sort them, guide them and advise them. Yet in unstandardised form they are likely to give misleading information, and injustice as well as mistakes can result. Yet a few elementary safeguards can remove most of the distortions.

The problem arises from the absence of a zero as a base from which marks can be given. With careful design it is possible to get equal intervals between grades on a scale for assessing performance, but each grade acquires meaning by relation to the rest, not to some nought as on a ruler. This is why we are norm-referencing. The best we can do is to compare the performance of one child with that of a group, but that raises the problem of what group is relevant. Is it the class, the year-group, all children in an LEA, some national sample, all the children who can read, and so on? Each comparison is likely to give a different result for the same performance by any one child. A good example of this can be found in any APU report by looking at the performance of children in metropolitan and in non-metropolitan areas. The latter always score lower on average than the former. Should comparisons for children in metropolitan areas be against national or metropolitan norms? Comparisons can be accidentally fixed to give flattering or critical results.

The relative nature of norm-referenced assessments means that they say nothing about absolute standards. It may be disgraceful, but half the pupils are always going to come below the average. They may all be first-class honours material, but only 25% are going to be in the top quarter. If decisions are going to be made on the basis of marks given, there should be control over both the average and the spread of marks, and this control should be exercised after agreement among all those teachers whose marks may be compared, for all the children where comparisons may be made. This means fixing the spread of marks arbitrarily, but it is likely to produce the least injustice. If there are serious doubts about the procedure that follows because a teacher claims that her class is superior or inferior and her marks should not be adjusted, the headteacher can be asked to adjudicate. As a further guide a common test, or better still, a common standardised verbal reasoning test could be used to test the claim that one class is better or worse than others. But the principle still applies: raw marks should not be made public without some standardisation.

Let us start with proud parents of a middle school child looking at the end-of-year report. For each subject teachers have given a percentage. Encouraged by the rather bland comments alongside the percentages the parents scan the attainments subject by subject.

| Mathematics | 71% | English | 55% |
| French | 50% | Science | 82% |

It is obvious that the strength is on the science side. But the parents do not know what these percentages mean. As there is no zero and no recognisable scale for the parents to use, they need further information before coming to conclusions about performance between subjects. If the average for French was 45% and for mathematics 70%, conclusions might be different. If the spread of marks for English was from 95 to 20 while in science it was from 85 to 75, the parents would have to think again. The logical way to present such assessments is to accept that they are referenced to norms. A number of steps towards defining the norms can be recommended.

(1) Make it clear which is the group within which the comparison is being made. Say whether it is the class, or the age group, and the number in the group chosen for reference.
(2) Get agreement among all teachers taking the year group and, preferably, across the whole school to use the same comparisons in (1) above. This will reduce the chance of teachers or parents misunderstanding assessments.
(3) Try to get all teachers to agree to the use of one form of quantitative assessment, whether letter grades or percentages.

(4) Try to get agreement among teachers to grade or mark within an agreed range and to an agreed average.

(5) If no agreement can be attained under (4) above, get teachers to include the average range of percentages or the distribution of grades, on reports or record cards.

It is not easy to get teachers to agree to some arbitrary standard of marking, even for records or reports. To settle on an average of 50 and that 10 per cent should be above 70 or below 30 will be opposed because each class is unique, and such a constraint is arbitrary. It may be easier to achieve some standardisation of marks after they have been given. Two methods, chosen because they avoid complicated mathematics, are illustrated below.

The first method is to convert the raw scores from teachers to percentile ranks. This rank gives a pupil's position in the group within which the norms have been agreed, whether the class or year group. Here the 60th percentile is the score above 59% of all scores and below 39%. To convert raw scores to percentiles the following steps should be followed:

Step 1: Rank all students from highest to lowest.

Pupil	A	B	C	D	...	X	Y	Z	Total 26
Rank	22	7	2	16	...	14	11	4	

Step 2: Convert these ranks into percentiles by using the formula

$$\text{Percentile rank} = \frac{100 \times (N + 1) - R}{N}$$

where N = number in the group
R = rank of each pupil.

So for pupil A the percentile rank is

$$100 \times \frac{(26 + 1) - 22}{26}$$

$$= 19$$

With large numbers, or where percentiles are adopted across the year groups, it is easiest to convert raw scores to percentiles using a graph (see Satterley, 1981, pp. 138–43).

Percentiles enable performances on different subjects to be compared. They are also easily understood by parents. However, they should not be added together or averaged. They should also not be used for comparing the performance of groups which are very contrasting in their attainment.

A second and mathematically superior way of preparing different sets of scores so that they can be compared is to convert each of them to a new common scale so that they have the same mean and standard deviation. The latter is a measure of the spread of marks around the mean (average mark), and if all marks can be converted to a common mean and standard deviation they will be comparable. This procedure of standardising marks has been simplified by the development of cheap calculators. Here the method suggested is to convert all scores into standard scores or standardised scores. The advantage of these is that all such scores reported to parents or used for important internal decisions about children are not only comparable, but can be added and averaged. This rests on the assumption that the spread of raw marks on each distribution is even about the mean in the form of a normal curve (see page 61), and not stacked up at the top or bottom. Lists of marks should be scrutinised for their spread before standardising.

It is unlikely that teachers will want to standardise many sets of test scores or other assessments. It will often be convenient for the standardisation to be carried out by a head or deputy. It is always necessary to check the procedure for using a calculator. The sequence of events can differ on different models, so follow instructions carefully.

To illustrate the procedure for standardising marks, the raw scores of two children, John and Jane, have been selected from assessments of English and mathematics. Their scores, extracted from those of all the children in their class, are as follows:

	John's raw score	Jane's raw score
English	56	65
Maths	70	60
Total	126	125

Now steps are taken to bring these scores to the same mean and standard deviation. For convenience a mean of 50 and a standard deviation of 10 have been selected. These would then be used to standardise all scores selected because of their importance for decision-making about the children. Comparisons could then be made because they were on the same base.

Step 1. Read the instructions for using the calculator to work out standard deviation. Complete this procedure for all the raw scores of the class or year-group on each test. In our example the standard deviations were 12 for English and 15 for mathematics. As a crude check for a class of 25–35, work our the range (top mark minus bottom mark) and divide this by 4. The answer should be within a few points of the calculated standard deviation.

Step 2. Use the calculator to find the mean or average for all the raw scores of the class or year-group in each test. In our example the means were 47 for English and 62.5 for mathematics.

Step 3. For each child, deduct the mean from the raw score and divide by the standard deviation. This gives a standard score. For John and Jane this works out as follows:

| | Raw Scores | | Whole Class | | Standard Score | |
	John	Jane	Mean	SD	John	Jane
English	56	65	47	12	$\frac{56-47}{12} = 0.75$	$\frac{65-47}{12} = 1.5$
Maths	70	60	62.5	15	$\frac{70-62.5}{15} = 0.5$	$\frac{60-62.5}{15} = -0.17$
Total	126	125				

Step 4. The standard scores above are now ready for use. But they are small and can be negative because their mean is zero. Hence we now convert them to our chosen mean of 50 and standard deviation of 10.

| | Raw Scores | | Standard Scores | | Standardised Scores | |
	John	Jane	John	Jane	John	Jane
English	56	65	0.75	1.5	$(0.75 \times 10) + 50$ $= 57.5$	$(1.5 \times 10) + 50$ $= 65$
Maths	70	60	0.5	−0.17	$(0.5 \times 10) + 50$ $= 55$	$(-0.17 \times 10) + 50$ $= 48.3$
Total	126	125	1.25	1.33	112.5	113.3

With these four steps carried out, a set ot scores is available that can be added, averaged and compared. It will be seen that the procedure has changed the interpretation that would be given to the relative performance of John and Jane. On the raw scores John seems slightly superior overall. Once the scores are standardised Jane has a slightly higher total. Furthermore, John, while apparently superior in maths when compared to English on raw scores, turns out to score higher on English when the comparison is on the same statistical base.

Finally, do not be over-confident in such procedures as standardisation. It produces a fairer basis for making decisions about children where assessment is involved. It ensures that comparisons are being made on the same mathematical basis. But there are assumptions behind the statistics that could still make the comparisons misleading. In particular, school class-sizes are small, and scores will rarely be spread normally, evenly, about the mean, and this undermines the basis of the calculations. Thus, it is safer to be cautious over small differences, and to look for other evidence to see if any conclusions are supported.

Self-referencing. Assessing progress over time is attractive but technically very complicated. The APU, for example, has been engaged in successive annual testing of mathematics, language and science to check whether standards are rising or falling. But while the testing was proceeding, so was the debate over the method chosen to monitor change over time. The Rasch technique was chosen by the National Foundation for Educational Research. Doubt was thrown on it by academics. Then the Department of Education and Science asked independent experts to comment on whether the technique would yield trends. Obviously, if the experts find assessment over time so difficult, the classroom teacher should not assume that collecting marks and comparing them will give reliable indications of academic progress. Once again, distinctions between assessment as objective and evaluation as subjective are misleading. Both are loaded with the values of those who design and use them.

Self-referencing is therefore an area for professional judgement. It is important to assess whether a pupil is improving or deteriorating. Sometimes the grades or marks given reflect a dramatic improvement or decline. Form positions may alter over the years. The 11-plus failure did occasionally become the star A-level pupil. The idler in the reception class may become the pace-maker of the top juniors. Stars dim and plodders sprint. It is important to assess to be in a position to do something about it. Furthermore, it is always necessary to distinguish effort from attainment in making such assessments over time.

Once again, prior definition is the key in assessing performance or effort over time. This can be related to content or to norms. It is useful to know that a pupil has progressed from 'Able to tell the time on the hours' to 'Able to tell the time in hours and minutes'! It is also useful to know that under the heading on the record card a child assessed on 'Produces work that is neat and tidy' has moved from 'Always' in the autumn term to 'Never' in the summer term. In each case there is a basis for action. The assessment is an *aide-mémoire* for the teacher or the next teacher and for parents. It ensures that selected changes are not overlooked.

Some teachers use improvement or deterioration to decide on borderline grades or marks. But any confusion of referencing is hazardous. The very able and industrious pupil has little room for improvement; the slacker can pick up a lot of credit at the crucial time by temporary effort. It is safer to keep self-referencing separate from other assessment of attainment, but there is no reason why pupils themselves should not be involved in it. It is good training for them to assess their own efforts and even to set their own targets for future performance. Part of the feedback to pupils should be an assessment of their industry, whether in relation to particular subjects or in relation to the rest of the class. Standards in games provide a typical example. Children as well as adults can set themselves targets in achieving specified times or distances. The content-referencing here is easy. You can or cannot high-jump 4 feet. You can set a target of 4 feet 6 inches, work at it and report at the end of the period. The now infrequently used form position can be used by children in this way. Challenged by a low position a child can set out to get near the top. Once again the ethical advantage of content-referencing is obvious. You improve your norm-referenced position by displacing others. Everyone can achieve more if achievement is referenced to content or standards.

Stage 3: Building into Teaching and Learning

Practice	*Structure by:*	*To produce:*
Content-referenced checklists, profiles, inventories. Norm-referenced tests and grades. Self-referenced reports.	Building into the organisation of learning and teaching in the classroom and throughout the school.	Feedback for pupils. Data for curriculum development. Record cards and reports for parents.

There is a danger, particularly at a time when teachers are being pressed to account for their use of scarce resources, for assessment to become an end in itself. There is always a danger of redundancy among the information that is collected. Record cards may rarely be used. Standardised tests may be used, but through routine rather than for the information they yield. Data may be passed on to secondary schools, yet not used when it arrives. Yet the justification of assessment primarily lies in its use in improving learning and only secondarily in the rendering of accounts. Even worse, there is an inertia in school affairs, and once the investment is made in producing information the procedure is likely to persist beyond the point where it is valuable to learning.

Thus one measure of effective assessment is the extent of use. The information obtained has to be planned to help children to learn and teachers to develop curricula. It should be pruned when it is no longer useful. The grossly over-simplified early models of curriculum development were based on this model.

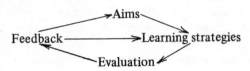

Now it is obviously absurd to model in this way with the suggestion of a cycle of continuous improvement through feedback. Yet this is the intuitive model used by teachers. If it were not, professional pride and confidence in schooling would soon evaporate. The model is applied intuitively by teachers because it is necessary to adapt even to maintain current effectiveness. This is why assessment is an integral part of teaching. Thus, this model can be used to establish the place of assessment. The feedback goes to pupils, other teachers, headteachers, parents, sometimes LEAs and always to the teacher responsible. Most assessment can be left intuitive or unsystematic, but some must be planned into the organisation of the school, the classroom and into the relation between teachers, pupils and parents.

The organisation of assessment into school organisation is discussed in Part II. Recording, storing and retrieving the information for use is the subject of Chapter 5. Very often this aspect of assessment receives low priority. Teachers go through the motions of assessing, but make little use of the data collected. Yet this is really the central stage because it contains the assessment of assessment. The criterion for this assessment is utility. If it is useful, keep and develop it. If it is not used, prune it.

Stage 4: Improving Reliability and Validity

Practice	*Structure by:*	*To produce:*
Assessment built into the organisation of learning.	Reviewing reliability, validity and use.	Cost-effective integrated assessment used for internal decision-making and external relations.

Evaluation that is part of teaching is bound into the cycle of events through which teaching successes are preserved and failures rejected. This means that the three steps recommended early in this chapter are repeated as part of the planning of teaching. As information is produced on individual children its usefulness in the teaching process, the purposes it is fulfilling and its objectivity should be queried, using the questions introduced in this chapter.

There are a number of occasions that are particularly useful in the improvement of evaluation. The users of the information such as secondary school teachers or parents can provide their views on its relevance and validity. Taking second opinions and discussions among teachers about children can focus attention on weaknesses or strengths in evaluation. When standardised tests are used, the discrepancies between teacher evaluations and test scores can be examined. Teacher-made test design as discussed in the next chapter can be improved. Once again, improving reliability and validity is a matter of conceiving evaluation as part of teaching and as such, open to adaptation. Evaluation should be thought of as developing as teaching is developed.

A Teaching Model for Evaluation

We can now put all the stages together to give a model for assessment that links it to teaching. Any progress through the stages will improve the assessment. The emphasis has been on assessment as professional judgement rather than through the design of tests, or the use of published tests. These are important and are dealt with in Chapter 3. But even when no tests are used, teachers can benefit by considering evaluation as part of the way they organise learning for pupils. The model makes explicit the actions of the best teachers.

Structure 1	*Product 1*	*Structure 2*	*Product 2*
Select key curriculum aspects.	*Checkpoints* Transfer and grouping data	*Reference to:* (a) Content (b) Norms	(a) Checklists, inventories, profiles (b) Grades and test results for comparisons
		(c) Self	(c) Time series on individual attainment

Structure 3	*Product 3*	*Structure 4*	*Product 4*
Build into organisation of learning.	Feedback for pupils. Information for records, parents, teachers, etc.	*Improve* reliability, validity.	Evaluation for decisions.

3 CONSTRUCTING TESTS FOR ASSESSMENT

Following the plan to help develop existing teacher practices rather than recommending systematic assessment from first principles, this chapter will be mainly about the design of tests, but as *aide-mémoire*, lists of questions for improving what is already done, whether this is oral questioning or end-of-term examination, project and practical work, or the observation that is the basis of most running assessments. It has been assumed that results are to be used, whether by feeding back results to children or into planning of the curriculum or the organisation of learning, or through pupil-marked or evaluated exercises. There is a lot of wasted information in the education service. Every year public examinations are used to produce a grade, but not to feed information back to teachers. Wherever possible, information from assessment should be guiding pupils and staff so matters can be improved. It should not just be indicating the level of terminal performance.

It is clear why teachers design their own tests. They either cannot afford to buy published ones, or they do not have the time or the knowledge to find them, or cannot see them fitting what is going on in their classrooms. This may be because the content does not fit, or the level of difficulty is wrong, or the age-range is different. But it is also liable to be because the educational reasoning behind the test is suspect. Teachers who see reading as something that comes through understanding and enjoyment, see word-recognition tests as inadequate. Verbal reasoning tests may seem suitable for suburban, middle-class whites, but unfair to inner-city, working-class blacks. There is also a very limited range of published tests. The assessment of reading is an exception, yet even there teachers find it very difficult to choose tests that are relevant to their approach and their curriculum. The hard way to learn this lesson is to negotiate the use of a reading test for assessment across all schools with representative teachers and advisors from a local authority. Every one is an expert, and none of them agrees with anyone else.

Testing is therefore problematic. Published tests may be reliable, but in the context of the classroom, validity may be suspect. A solution is to design your own test, but there are problems here as well. The eight questions that follow are a guide to producing tests with reliability and validity.

Question 1: *Why do I want to test?*
This is a most useful first question. It removes the need for much further work in many cases. There is no point in an elaborate test for a simple purpose. Teachers often decide on a quick test to motivate pupils, or to bring them to order. 'You should find out as much as you can about this over the weekend and I will be asking you questions about it on Monday.' 'At the end of the week we are going to have a test on what we have learned about plants.' There is little point in investing a lot of time in the motivational tests that follow. The important point is that they should not put pupils off their work. Even if used to restore order they should not be boring or beyond some of the children. If tests are to be ends in themselves or to support teaching, they should at least encourage the children. The care taken over design should not remove the fun that can be obtained from a session on multiplication tables or spelling.

Once the purpose of testing is to find out what has been learned, to see whether the underlying content has been understood and the skills mastered, or to select among pupils, care has to be taken or the decisions made may be mistaken. But there is another purpose that lies behind much testing. This is to emphasise what is important. The test defines for pupils what seems to be given priority in the mind of the teacher. Many of the tips come through oral or written tests that may have little reliability or validity, yet still manage to define priorities. It seems curious that pupils have to obtain clues in this indirect way and, as with tests for motivation, it might be better to solve the problem another way through making it clear what is important. But tests are used for this purpose. The professional advice to the APU was to include tricky areas such as personal and social development for consideration for national testing because they are important to teachers, and if not tested might be devalued. In the end the decision was not to assess this area.

We are left with testing for mastery of content or to differentiate among pupils or to assess progress. Sorting these purposes out determines whether tests are to be content-referenced, and therefore designed to see whether content has been mastered or not, or norm-referenced, where the aim is to spread children out so that differentiating between them is easier, or self-referenced so that performance on one test can be compared with that taken previously.

Question 2: *What use is to be made of the results?*
Here is another question that can save work. If the results are to be

ignored there is little point in using a test that is expensive of time or money. For example, homework that is in the form of a test is not always marked or even looked at. Neither are a lot of the essays or exercises set in class. The assumption behind such work is that the pupil will benefit from completing it. It is an end in itself. In many of these cases more benefit would be derived if pupils were to assess their own work. In some cases they can usefully assess each other's work. The teacher's task is to organise the testing so that this self-assessment is rewarding. Once again assessment merges into teaching; what is got out depends on what is planned in.

If the results are to be used for finding out where children are in their learning, or how they differ from one another, then they are important, and reliability and validity matter. Then there has to be more investment of time and thought. The implicit assessments used by all teachers need to be made explicit. But there are degrees of importance. Any evidence to parents, or to other teachers, on children needs to be produced with more care than information that is for immediate guidance in the classroom, where it is supported by the teacher's knowledge of the class. Evidence made public is also restricted in scope by the space on the report or the record card or the brevity of the interview with parents. It has to be dependable because a lot of weight can be placed on a little evidence. In continuous assessment in the classroom there should be a flow of evidence from many different techniques and sources. The teacher organises this flow of information to assess children, sort them out to match the curriculum to the individual and give them an idea of how they are doing. Each item should be as dependable as possible; but it is the accumulation that matters. The weight placed on any one item is reduced.

This rather cavalier approach to assessment, suggesting that assessment can be selective to save effort, is nevertheless realistic. Teachers are too busy to design every test on lines recommended in manuals on assessment. Questions 1 and 2 are guides to economy of effort, whether in design or marking. But this also applies to recording and storing data. Asking these questions is the first step to a clean-out of unused information. This is why record cards in a permanent, inflexible format can be a nuisance. The titles fix the data to be collected across years when much of it becomes redundant. Meanwhile crucial information is missing.

Question 3: *Which are the important things to assess?*
This question completes the pruning that precedes thinking about the design of tests. Obviously not everything can or should be assessed;

much assessment can be left at the impressionistic level. But just as a model of assessment has to include selection to concentrate on the central core of work without which later learning would founder, so it is necessary to concentrate any time available for carefully planned testing on the areas of work that must be mastered, or where information is needed for important decisions about children.

The repetition of this point throughout this book is deliberate. The resistance to systematic assessment from teachers is usually manifested in the question 'If I assess as thoroughly as you suggest, what time will I have left over for teaching?' It becomes a serious problem when local authorities are encouraging or asking schools for self-assessments. The APU takes more of the available time through its test programmes, and information has to be prepared for parents and the public, following the 1980 Education Act. Governors are asking for more information. Any priority for assessment has to be established in the face of these demands. Thus the stress here on the need for parsimony.

Question 4: *What am I trying to achieve?*

Here we are again with objectives. They may accentuate the trivial or the measurable, and canalise learning towards pre-specified ends; but they are necessary as guides in even the most free-wheeling session. The question about ends remains central to assessment as it is to teaching. But to struggle from the admirable aims of producing good citizens, sensitive souls and moral human beings to objectives that can serve as the bases of testing, has exhausted many a persistent school staff. This has become a familiar and not necessarily rewarding occupation as teachers are persuaded to become accountable through producing accounts.

Fortunately a lot of the work has already been done by Bloom in his taxonomy (Bloom, 1956). This formidable-sounding instrument is nothing but a classification of learning skills. It is useful because it ranks learning objectives or skills. Thus, the six levels of the taxonomy are of increasing complexity, and for intellectual, cognitive assessment the following six levels of skill are suggested. While each is further sub-divided, these major categories are sufficient to help teachers to set objectives in terms of skills that go beyond just knowing about things.

Knowledge – being able to recall, describe, define
Comprehension – being able to explain in own words, illustrate, interpret, generalise
Application – being able to apply, develop, transfer

Analysis — being able to classify, distinguish, detect
Synthesis — being able to relate, organise, derive
Evaluation — being able to judge, compare, contrast

Similar taxonomies have been developed for affective and experiential objectives (Kratwohl, 1964; Steinaker and Bell, 1975).
Once the purpose is to choose guides to what to assess rather than to settle on
measurable outcomes, it is the broad headings rather than the detail
that are useful. The taxonomy suggests that broad and deep aspects of
learning can be assessed. The six categories above go beyond recall of
facts towards more profound skills that have more general application.
Countless working parties in such organisations as the Schools Council
planning curriculum development, or in the APU planning assessment
have been grateful to Bloom for this *aide-mémoire*. Essentially the
teacher planning a test is asking, 'Can they recall, interpret, categorise
and so on?' It is their ability to do things and use them that should be
assessed. The six levels are ways into testing what skills have been
learned. But these skills are used to master content. Any classroom
learning consists of content as well as skills. Thus, it is helpful in
thinking about testing to picture two dimensions: skills and content.

Question 5: *What content should be covered?*
This question extends the selectivity suggested in Question 3. Once
objectives, however broad, have been made explicit, the work to be
covered has to be thought out. Objectives and content are brought
together before considering how to assess them, and this is best done by
producing a test plan (sometimes referred to as a test blueprint). Most
writers on assessment recommend something like the following,
suggested here for a topic on health education.

OBJECTIVES	CONTENT		
	Action for Health	*Nutrition*	*Diseases*
Knowledge of	Diet Exercise Sleep Cleanliness	Proteins Carbohydrates Vitamins	Communicable Non-communicable
Comprehension of	Digestion Calories	Balanced diet	Immunisation Body defences

This plan can be used to ensure that all the important content has
been sampled in the test, and that the objectives beyond simple recall
have been covered.

Here is a table of objectives produced in the curriculum areas of history, geography and social science (Cooper, 1976, p. 10). Testing would be based on such a list, illustrated through content in specific contexts.

SKILLS			PERSONAL QUALITIES
Intellectual	*Social*	*Physical*	*Interests, Attitudes, Values*
1. The ability to find information from a variety of sources, in a variety of ways. 2. The ability to communicate findings through an appropriate medium. 3. The ability to interpret pictures, charts, graphs, maps, etc. 4. The ability to evaluate information. 5. The ability to organise information through concepts and generalisations. 6. The ability to formulate and test hypotheses and generalisations.	1. The ability to participate within small groups. 2. An awareness of significant groups within the community and the wider society. 3. A developing understanding of how individuals relate to such groups. 4. A willingness to consider participating constructively in the activities associated with these groups. 5. The ability to exercise empathy (i.e. the capacity to imagine accurately what it might be like to be someone else).	1. The ability to manipulate equipment. 2. The ability to manipulate equipment to find and communicate information. 3. The ability to explore the expressive powers of the human body to communicate ideas and feelings. 4. The ability to plan and execute expressive activities to communicate ideas and feelings.	1. The fostering of curiosity through the encouragement of questions. 2. The fostering of a wariness of over-commitment to one framework of explanation and the possible distortion of facts and the omission of evidence. 3. The fostering of a willingness to explore personal attitudes and values to relate these to other people. 4. The encouraging of an openness to the possibility of change in attitudes and values. 5. The encouragement of worthwhile and developing interests in human affairs.

Question 6: *What types of test should I design?*

There are two types of test. In the first the answers are pre-specified; in the others answers can only be judged after production. The first are often labelled 'objective' because there is no question of having to judge an answer right or wrong. The answer is fixed in advance. In the second type of test essays or short answers are written, or oral answers given, and the teacher judges how well the question has been answered. Both involve judgement, one at the design stage, the other at the marking stage. Hence the term 'objective test' can be misleading. Furthermore, the 'objectivity' is obtained at the cost of reducing divergent responses. Essay-type questions are rightly popular because they allow pupils to expand their views, but their assessment can still be checked to increase the reliability of assessment without disturbing the chance for the exercise of imagination and individuality.

The first answer to the question comes from this commonsense about whether answers should be restricted in advance. If not, then essay-type questions should be set. But if pre-specification is not a distortion through restriction of options for answers, then assessment can be made more reliable by setting objective type tests. A glance back at the headings of Bloom's taxonomy will show that objective-type tests are more appropriate at the 'knowledge' level. Inevitably, essay-type questions or practical exercises will be necessary to assess the ability to evaluate or synthesise. Similarly, it may be easy to organise activities of a structured kind to test objectively physical achievements such as swimming a length of the swimming bath, or tying a reef knot. But it is more likely to be appropriate to set open-ended activities so as to be able to judge aesthetic appreciation or artistic feelings, and to judge the end-product, argument or activity by using professional judgement. Do not strangle the imagination in an assessment noose!

The second answer is to decide on the basis of the sampling of skills and content that is needed. If it is essential to test that many key skills have been learned, or facts absorbed, then objective-type tests are best. The structured answers mean that a lot of ground can be covered in a short time, but if sampling across a wide range of work is less important than assessing a few areas in depth, essay-type answers will probably yield more illuminating answers. Both types of test yield useful information for teaching purposes, and a combination is often best. It is as important to know which key areas have not been mastered as it is to see whether pupils are developing the ability to develop sophisticated ideas and complex skills.

Question 7: *If I choose to use essay-type tests, how do I go about designing them?*

Essay-type questions allow scope for pupils to organise knowledge to tackle new problems. Their open-endedness allows for originality and imagination, so there is little point in using them to test the recall of factual information. But the opportunity for originality and divergence creates problems in marking. Since the 1920s there has been evidence showing wide variations in the marks given to essay-type examination answers. The best hope of reducing this unreliability is to follow a few guidelines to ensure that the question set gives students a clear idea of what ground is to be covered and at the same time to give a basis for assessing the answer. Divergence can be encouraged, but around a clearly defined area of content.

(1) Use a test plan as in the answer to Question 5, so that you have a clear idea of the type of answer you expect and the sort of thinking that you hope that the pupil will use. Very general titles that give no guidance will not help the pupils and will be difficult to mark. If the thinking that is being encouraged is complicated, suggest subheadings in the title. If it is to be imaginative, give the base from which the imagination is to take off. Above all, the task set should not be ambiguous. Pupils should not have to guess what is meant. The title or question should define the task.

(2) With primary and middle school children do not expect long answers. It is better to set a number of shorter exercises until practice in essay writing is developed.

(3) If essay-type questions are asked in the form of a test, allow time for the weaker to finish. If the ability to work against the clock is being tested, short-answer questions should be used. But give time to think and plan an answer.

(4) If essay-type questions are asked in the form of a test, vary the difficulty of questions to give the able scope for developing sophisticated answers while allowing the less able to do their best.

(5) Decide in advance whether you are going to mark analytically, through the use of a checklist of important points, or impressionistically covering the whole essay or some combination of both. The answer to the balance between these approaches to marking depends on the purpose of the test. If it is to check mastery of key skills, then analytical marking will be given priority. If it is to allow scope for developing ideas then holistic, overall marking will dominate. In each case the qualities to be looked for should be decided in advance, when the titles or questions are set.

(6) Use comments on returned essays to help pupils to develop techniques, correct faults and extend strengths. Reference grades to content, criteria or previous performance as discussed in Chapter 2, so that pupils know what their grade means, if that is the purpose of the exercise.

(7) Think out how essays are to be marked in advance. This will help improve reliability in marking and also illuminate weaknesses in the essay title or question.

Question 8: *If I choose objective-type tests, how do I go about designing them?*

Once again the start of designing objective-type tests is a plan covering the areas to be tested. Items will be written to sample each important area of the work to be tested. Because answers are short, often a word, an underlining or a number, a lot of work can be sampled by such tests. But the simplicity of objective-type items can conceal as much ambiguity as an essay question. The items may not reflect the knowledge and skills that the teacher intended. They may be too easy or too difficult for the pupils. The items need examination to ensure that they are reliable and valid. An idea of the difficulty of doing the necessary analysis can be gauged from the attempts of the statisticians advising the APU to agree on the Rasch method of measuring performance over time. The method assumes that only the ability of the children and the difficulty of the item determine performance on a test item. It is assumed that the teaching received does not influence the difficulty encountered. This issue remains in dispute, and it would be ridiculous to expect teachers to carry out item analyses to improve tests when the techniques are not only complicated but there is no agreement among experts. An excellent and practical source for those interested in designing objective-type tests has been produced by Satterley (1981).

Examples of pencil-and-paper objective questions can be found in any publication of Assessment of Performance testing, or in published objective tests. The questions are 'objective' because there is no interpretation needed to mark and answer right or wrong. Two broad types can be distinguished: restricted response and structured response.

Restricted-response items
These can ask for simple recall or for the completion of statements as follows.
These are recall items:
   'In which year did the Second World War end?'
   'What is the product of 7 times 9?'
These are completion items:
   'Water consists of molecules of hydrogen and . . .'
   'If 7 times X = 56, then X = . . .'

These questions are easy to construct and useful for testing 'knowledge of' questions, particularly in mathematics and science. There are a few 'do and don't' hints in writing them:

(1) The answers should be about important aspects, not trivia.
(2) The question should call for only one specific, unambiguous answer.
(3) In completion types put the blanks at or near the end of the statement.
(4) In numerical questions indicate the units for the answer.
(5) Omit only key words in completion types, and keep the statement short with few blanks.
(6) Group items covering the same content together.
(7) Group together the recall and the completion-type items.
(8) Score items either 0 or 1, as each question should have led to such unambiguous scoring.
(9) Practise, revise and edit.

Structured-response items
These can be true/false or multiple choice in structure as follows:
'If food is frozen, harmful bacteria are killed.' True or false?
'Influenza is caused by viruses.' True or false?
These are true/false (alternative response) items. Answers are usually indicated by underlining.
'Who was Prime Minister during the Battle of Britain?'
(a) Chamberlain   (d) Churchill
(b) Baldwin   (e) Eden
'What is 40 per cent as a fraction?'
(a) $\frac{2}{5}$ (b) $\frac{4}{5}$ (c) $\frac{1}{2}$ (d) $\frac{4}{11}$

Multiple-choice items can be designed to examine higher-level skills such as comprehension, application, analysis, synthesis or evaluation, apart from examining knowledge. But their flexibility can easily lead to misleading 'stems' of questions, or options for answers that are not clearly right or wrong. The 'stem' should define the task or problem. There are a few 'do and don't' hints in writing them:

(1) The instructions must be clear. Answering such questions is a technique that has to be learned, and young children need careful guidance. They must know what to do.
(2) Make answer choices short by formulating a clear problem or question in the stem.
(3) Keep answer choices the same length to avoid the pupil jumping at the longest or shortest because it stands out.
(4) Avoid negatives in the statement of the problem or question.

(5) Make all possible answers plausible, but make 'distractors' (deliberately wrong answers) clearly incorrect.

(6) Be sure that there is only one correct answer.

(7) Include a 'none of these answers above' or 'all of the above' if appropriate, but use these infrequently.

(8) Avoid including clues to the right answer in the stem.

(9) Practise, revise and edit.

Restricted and structured response tests can sample a wide range of work and involve children in deep thinking. Multiple-choice questions in particular can probe into understanding. Below, for example, are two questions from the APU's *Science in Schools. Age 11, Report No. 1* (HMSO, 1981).

Multiple-choice items are particularly useful for assessing content and skills of varying complexity. Scoring them is easy, and they can also be fun. But they can be shallow, and if there are few questions they are open to guessing. This is why a mix of essay and objective-type tests is usually preferable; but the latter can yield information for pupil and teacher for immediate use in deciding where to go next. A quick run through the proportion of children getting each item right can show where further work is necessary. Those failing at items that most get right can be identified. Every teacher realises this potential of short-answer tests, whether written or oral for a quick identification of the grasp attained and the proportion getting it right. Once again, the recommendation is to concentrate on improving tests which can be

Question page

Look at this picture of an apple tree in a field.

Read the statements below.
Tick the one which you can be most sure is true just by looking at the picture.

☐ The wind has knocked some apples off the tree

☐ There are apples on the ground and on the tree

☐ The apples on the tree are ready for picking

☐ The apples on the ground are bad

☐ The tree could not hold all its apples

Comment
There is a degree of inference in making any observation and here the pupils were being asked to pick out the statement where least assumptions were being made. In this question it is the second statement which requires the fewest assumptions in order to be judged as true. The results shown below under-estimate the frequencies with which the distractors were chosen because of the high rate of multiple choice. Some incorrect statements were chosen more frequently than is shown but as part of multiple response.

Source: APU, 1981, p. 91. Reproduced with the permission of the Controller of Her Majesty's Stationery Office.

Question page

These are all stages in the life of a frog, but they are jumbled up.

Comment
The question requires application of the broad idea that the life cycle is always the same for a particular living thing. Giving the correct answer also depends upon recognising these parts of the frog's life cycle and knowing their order.

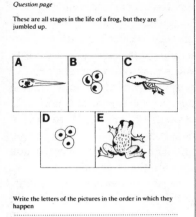

Write the letters of the pictures in the order in which they happen

....

Source: APU, 1981, p. 95. Reproduced with the permission of the Controller of Her Majesty's Stationery Office.

used repeatedly because they yield a lot of information and give reliable results. We all use objective tests in the classroom. Some are worth improving.

Improving Tests

Once a test has been designed it can be improved by a few simple steps. Once again, the statistical checks have been omitted although they are important (see Satterley, 1981). However, a lot can be done by keeping an eye on the way the test is taken and answered.

(1) Use each testing as a pilot study. In a world dedicated to good assessment each test would be tried out in advance on a sample of children similar to those for whom the test is ultimately destined. In practice teachers are unlikely to do this, so use every testing as a trial. If children question instructions, say they don't understand what to do, finish too soon or never finish, start chattering or make the test into paper darts, there is possibly something wrong. They will soon tell you what this is.

(2) Look through the answers. If all get the answers to a question right or wrong it is not discriminating. If the aim is to differentiate between the children, a range of 40 to 60 per cent correct is about right. If the aim is a test that has something for everyone and will spread

children out, settle for a range of correct answers of between 30 and 70 per cent for each question.

(3) Look at the distribution of answers for each question. There may be a consistent pattern among the wrong answers, suggesting general misunderstanding or a badly designed question. Look at the type of question that gets a high proportion of right answers. It is common in a subject like mathematics to find that mechanical skills are well learned, but that the application of skills is harder to master. Teachers can learn a lot through such a post-mortem.

(4) Give the test back to the pupils and take time to use it as a teaching aid, unless it is to be used again with the same children.

(5) Tests can be duplicated and the answers written on separate sheets. Once the test is improved and in a satisfactory form it can be stored for further use. But be careful that clear instructions are given for answers to be written on to the answer sheets. Objective tests depend on clear and standard instructions.

Teacher-made Tests in Use

It has been a recurring theme of this book that the key to improved and useful assessment in schools lies in approaches through models rather than in more reliable tests. Furthermore, the amount of assessment through formal tests is in practice very small. Most assessment takes place through observation during teaching, and through written or oral testing that occurs because it fits into a particular sequence of learning. Teachers often write a test on the board or take a question-and-answer session without much planning. As the purpose of this assessment is to gauge progress and plan the next steps, this is an essential part of teaching. Formal testing will be rare, and that tested will be selected because it is central to further learning.

This can be illustrated by considering the assessment instruments in use in a typical primary school. First, there are record cards requiring teachers to grade children on important skills or to describe their attainments, or to place them into categories specified on the record. Most of the evidence for filling in this record will be accumulated from observations and informal assessments, not carefully designed tests. There may be a space for results of standardised tests in reading and possibly in mathematics, but the major part will be devoted to judgements of the teacher through knowledge of the child in question. Even where formal tests have been set, the results will probably have been used to complete a running record kept by the teacher rather than being entered directly on to the record. Similarly, checklists, inventories and profiles will be completed from knowledge accumulated by the teacher, using test results where available. There is very little formal testing in most primary or middle schools, and that which is organised is added to other assessments for later use.

Is it worth the trouble to design reliable and valid tests given this indirect influence of the results? Inevitably, test results will be judged as valid against the many judgements made by teachers on children. But that does not diminish the importance of taking care over the testing of key aspects of learning. The more care that is taken, the more the results can add to the other assessments made. Indeed, it is when test results contrast with teacher judgements that genuine educational issues arise. Feeding standardised scores of reading back to primary schools in Inner London in the 1970s often produced letters pointing out that the external results received conflicted with those collected internally, whether through testing or through the judgement of the staff. The consequent exchange of views usually revolved around the different aspects of reading assessed by the external test, the different conditions under which the results were obtained, the bases for comparisons used by teachers within the school, and so on. One of the reasons for using most standardised tests is that they have national norms. Teachers often use norms established within their own experience in a single school, or by impressionistic comparison with nearby schools, or by looking at inner-city or rural schools rather than those across the nation. The more care that is taken over the design of a test, the more confidently it can be used to enrich the evidence accumulated for finally deciding on the attainment of a pupil or a school in some specific area of work.

Thus, the distinction between testing that is immediate, an ongoing part of a lesson, an on-the-spot guide to progress and planning on the one hand, and testing that is carefully thought out, tried out and progressively improved, should be maintained. Both have their place, and they should not be confused. But both impressionistic and objective assessments play a complementary part. One reason why teachers ignore most books on assessment is that the work involved in implementing the technical suggestions is not only formidable, but would be exhausting if this formal assessment stood by itself. In reality it is only a very small part of total assessment that needs careful design, retrospective analysis and, if norm-referenced, standardised marking procedures.

Finally, as indicated in Chapter 2, any progress towards reliable and valid tests for crucial areas of work is worthwhile. Get as far as you can in putting into practice the answers to the questions in this chapter. There are three practical steps that often help:

(1) Prepare the test plan described in Question 5 as you prepare the teaching for the topic. Then keep it in mind for any informal testing as well as in the design of any formal tests.

(2) Prepare the tests in advance and look at them again before use. The second look will often do more good than a lot of technical sophistication.

(3) If results are to be norm-referenced there will have to be some standardisation, even if it is just agreement to use roughly the same average and spread of marks. But here, and more particularly with content-referenced tests that are dividing children into those who have, or have not, mastered key areas of work, take second opinions of the reliability and validity of the tests. Two or more professional heads are better than one.

4 PUBLISHED TESTS AND INVENTORIES

In Chapter 3 the difficulties in constructing bespoke tests were outlined. Obviously it saves teacher time if tests can be bought ready-made. This is obviously easier if there is some common, standard part of the curriculum. A country where the Ministry of Education dictated the curriculum and provided the textbooks could ensure that teachers could have standardised content and norm-referenced tests to sequence children through the work and to sort them out by their relative attainment. With our arrangements, teachers have difficulty in finding published tests that match the curriculum they themselves design. The tests rarely seem valid. There is gain in this as well as loss. It is difficult to impose testing on to schools when there is variety in the curriculum; but the chance of the tests distorting the curriculum via teaching to the test, or of tests measuring aspects not covered by the children tested is increased.

In this chapter norm-referenced tests are dealt with first. These are designed to spread out children in order to discriminate between them. Then published content-referenced instruments are described. These are designed to sort out children according to their success in mastering content. Throughout, the warning in Chapter 1 has to be remembered: tests should never be the sole basis for discussions about children; they are one source of information only. This applies particularly to published tests, because their content is unlikely to match that taught in any one classroom, or their rationale to match that of any one teacher. This caution applies to all types of published test. For example, criterion-referenced tests such as the *Thackray Reading Readiness Profiles* (1973) for the 4 and 5-year-olds, or the *Get Reading Right Test* (1971), a phonic test for any ages, are based on listing reading skills. But lists of skills may have little to do with the way reading skill is actually acquired (Vincent and Cresswell, 1976). In the end teachers have to interpret test results. That professional judgement is best exercised before and after published tests are used.

Published tests, whether of attainments, intelligence or personality, are standardised. This term covers three qualities. First, they are constructed by a series of trials, analyses and revisions by experienced test-constructors. Or rather, they should be. In this country the National Foundation for Educational Research (NFER) is the major test-construction agency, and their copyright offers some guarantee of careful preparation. There are recognised procedures for collecting together items, sampling from this pool, conducting a pilot run, analysis of results and a re-run of these steps to improve reliability and validity.

The care taken over the design of tests varies. The *Culture Fair Tests* were originally constructed by Cattell while he was working with Spearman on 'g' factor intelligence in the 1930s (Institute for Personality and Ability Testing, 1973). Since then they have gone through several revisions to ensure that the items used were the best available and that they had not become redundant. At each stage samples of thousands were used to get data on the items and the tests as a whole. But there are also published tests where very little care has been taken over design, and where there has been no effort at updating. A simple rule can be applied: if the test manual which describes how the test should be used does not include a description of how and when it was constructed, it should be treated with suspicion.

The second aspect of standardisation is that there should be explicit procedures for administering and marking the test. The best tests often have apparently fussy instructions that involve stop watches, spare pencils, rigid adherence to the words in the given instructions and so on. But that is usually a sign that the designers are concerned that the testing should be under standard conditions, particularly where the results are to be norm-referenced. But the scoring is also standardised by being objective, and nothing is left to the interpretation of the marker. Answers are right or wrong and where there is latitude, this is spelled out in the manual of instructions. This can result in apparently daft answers being scored as right. But the test has been constructed on trial runs with large numbers of children, and the user should not buy a standardised test and play fast-and-loose with it.

Finally, published tests, which are usually norm-referenced, have tables of norms which enable any one person taking the test to be compared with the large group on which the test was standardised. Usually the score of the tested is found in the table opposite his or her age, and a standardised score read off the other axis. This standardised score for most tests published in England has a mean of 100 and a spread (standard deviation) around that mean of 15. Reading age or intelligence quotients are other forms of standardised score.

Standardised tests are the nearest instrument available to teachers approximating to the standard tests used by doctors. Both involve following standard procedures in application. There is a close parallel in the way both have been developed. The probability that a patient has a disease after the doctor has applied a standard test is based on the accumulated results from representative samples of the population. Similarly, an individual child's score on an attainment test is referenced to the scores from the sample used to standardise the test. In both cases the confidence in the assessment depends on reference to evidence that is independent of the doctor or teacher using the test.

There are, however, obvious differences in the two cases. The medical reference is to symptoms that give a degree of confidence that a disease is present, based on the proportion in the sample on which the test was developed who were found to have the disease. It is criterion-referenced. Most standardised tests in education are norm-referenced to the performance of a large sample used to standardise, but not to the content actually mastered. The external reference accounts for the weight placed on such tests. Doctor and teacher can be secure in obtaining a detached assessment because of the conditions under which the test was designed and implemented.

The limitations of such measures from tests are, however, well documented in both medicine and education. Here the concern is with the way they are used. When a doctor begins his search for the trouble he listens to the patient's complaints, asks questions about the problem, builds up a history of the case, refers this to records from his files, inspects the relevant part of the body, touches, listens and observes. Then he may carry out a standard test. But while the colour of the urine, or the blood pressure, or the chemical constitution of some body fluid may be telling evidence, the observation, interviewing and examination goes on. The test result is only one part of the assessment. It gives the doctor an often-known degree of confidence that this is jaundice and so on. But it is the combination of his various investigations that produces the diagnosis and the treatment.

In a medical examination there is also the possibility that the doctor's observation, the case history and the descriptions given by the patient, may all conflict with the evidence given by a test. No doctor would automatically assume that the test had given the objective evidence and that his diagnosis was wrong. Yet in education this often occurs. Indeed, the use of the term 'objective test' suggests that it is an assessment superior to subjective professional judgement.

The objectivity of tests is often assumed by researchers. Thus, the *Extending Beginning Reading* Schools Council Project (Southgate, Arnold and Johnson, 1981) involved the use of the Schonell Graded Word Reading Test. This test is the most widely used in schools, despite Schonell's own cautions about its capacity to measure 'real reading' (Schonell, 1945, p. 211). In the research project this test is used to judge the accuracy of teachers' accuracy in estimating their children's reading ability. Yet as Stierer (1982) has pointed out, the assumption is that the test provides a measure of reading performance against which teachers' estimates can be evaluated. Stierer quite reasonably asks why the test is taken as the true measure given the doubts about its validity. It would be more reasonable to evaluate the test against the professional judgement of the teachers.

When headteachers were asked, as part of the Evaluation and Testing in Schools Project, how they responded to objective test scores for children that were not those expected, they tended to favour their own judgement and reject the test scores (Steadman and Goldstein, 1982). Only 6 per cent of headteachers accepted the test score as right whether higher or lower than expected, and 12 per cent disbelieved the test in both situations. Only 15 per cent said that they would reconsider their own assessment in both cases. They were confident in their own knowledge of the children and sceptical of the test scores.

In education, tests have often obtained a status beyond that in medicine. They were used to select children for special education, for streams, for different types of secondary schools, for reporting to other teachers and to parents and employers. They are often used by central government through the APU, or LEAs through the advisors or inspectors, or by researchers, to yield evidence unsupported by other evidence. Teachers often use them as independent measures of a child's performance. Selection procedures for secondary schooling often involved assessment by teachers as well as tests. But the tests did attain a position of apparent objectivity that was not based on their reliability or validity. They yielded a score that had meaning only in relation to the group on which the test had been standardised. A score always had to be interpreted as open to the effects of coaching and to unusual circumstances during the testing. In addition, the test used might not have been appropriate for the children, and in all cases a tolerance should have been allowed a score because of the possibility that the sample used in the construction of the test was not representative of the population from which it was drawn.

A second reason for caution arose from the assumptions behind the construction of most tests. Achievements in reading, or mathematics and so on, or intelligence, or verbal reasoning, or even personality, were assumed to be stable, general attributes independent of the immediate context in which they could be assessed. A score on a test was assumed to indicate a competence that would be carried into all situations by the pupil, and could thus be used to place him in the appropriate group or school, or to give him work at the right level. That confidence among psychologists in the stability of attainments and of intelligence or personality has now evaporated.

These cautions will delight any sceptical teacher now in middle age, for in most cases they were right and the experts wrong over the reliability and validity of testing. This does not destroy the usefulness of standardised tests; they remain the most reliable instruments we have. But the fallible assumptions and the flaws in test design reinforce the view taken in this book: assessment should be part of teaching. If the results of standardised tests are used they should be one set of evidence among many. Like the doctor, the teacher should continue, in assessment, to employ observation, talking to children, listening to them, marking their written work. This, and discussion with pupils and with other staff, can gather up evidence that can be put alongside that from tests to form a judgement. Standardised tests are useful in the classroom, but they are not infallible. They are one part of the spectrum of assessment.

Why then do teachers pay for and use published tests? Mainly because this standardisation enables important questions to be answered. Through the norm-referencing teachers can see how their children or a particular group or individual compares with the wider group on which the test was standardised. Such tests can also give some idea of progress, although they have to be treated with caution. The tests can be used to form teaching groups, and to adjust tasks and materials to the different abilities of the children.

The problems with standardised tests start with the rarity with which they sample the curriculum organised within a particular school. Only in the testing of reading are there sufficient tests to give teachers a wide choice. These reading tests will be taken to illustrate the difficulties that can arise.

Testing What Aspect of Reading?

Tests have been designed to assess very different aspects of reading. Even concentrating on tests of reading attainment there is a wide variety to be found. Many of the most popular are word-recognition tests. The Young Group Reading Test, The Carver Word Recognition Test, The Burt Word Reading Test, The Schonell Graded Word Recognition Test all involve the pupil in selecting words spoken by the teacher, reading words aloud, or matching words to pictures. Many other popular tests involve pupils in completing sentences. These include the NFER tests A, AD and BD, the Daniels and Diack Graded Test of Reading and the Southgate Group Reading Test. Others involve pupils in continuous prose-reading followed by questions. Tests here include NFER Tests DE, EH2, the Schonell Reading Test R2 and R3, and the Neale Analysis of Reading Ability.

Another indication of the range of skills that can be tested under the umbrella of reading can be gauged from a test battery such as the Edinburgh Reading Tests. The Stage 3 of this test for 10.00 to 12.60 ages covers reading for facts, comprehension of sequences, retention through recall, comprehension of points of view and vocabulary. Each skill is tested through different methods. Thus, vocabulary is tested by completing sentences, selecting synonyms, familiarity with common phrases and by selecting to complete a précis. Thus, there are not only a variety of skills covered by the tests, but each involves the pupils in different activities. The teacher has to decide not only what aspect is to be tested, but how it is best tested.

Yielding What Kind of Score?

Regardless of the way a standardised test is constructed, and whatever aspect of attainment it measures, the raw score — the number of items answered correctly — has to be referenced to the performance of others who made up the group on which it was standardised. The simplest method was used in most early reading tests and produced a 'reading age'. Groups of different ages of children were given the test, and an item passed and failed by half a group was given the reading age of that group. This score is easy to interpret when the reading age is equal to the chronological age. The child is clearly average. But it can be a misleading indicator when the two ages do not coincide. The gap between chronological and reading age may mean something different at different ages. But even more misleading is the concept of a reading age itself. It suggests a smooth development as children get older. In practice development may be irregular and prediction is hazardous. Reading age too easily becomes a label.

The same criticisms apply to the 'reading quotient', because it uses the formula

$$\frac{\text{Reading Age}}{\text{Chronological Age}} \times 100$$

The child with a quotient of 100 has a reading age equal to his or her chronological age. But there is still the chance that retardation or advanced reading are misleadingly indicated by the quotient because of the different distributions of scores in the different samples used to produce the original reading ages.

Increasingly the 'standardised score' has come to be used in scoring reading tests. Here the mean of the group on which the test is standardised is fixed, usually at 100. The items are chosen to produce as near as possible a perfect, bell-shaped, normal curve as is illustrated below. Within this curve 68 per cent of all cases fall within plus or minus one

Figure 4.1: Normal Curve (Mean = 100, standard deviation (SD) = 15)

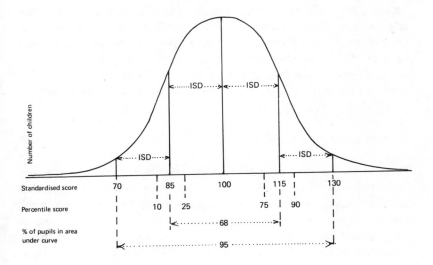

standard deviation (a measure of the spread of scores around the mean). In most British tests this standard deviation is fixed at 15, so that just over two-thirds of all cases will fall within the range 85 to 115. Similarly, 95 per cent will fall between 70 and 130. Thus, 2.5 per cent will be expected to score over 130, and 2.5 below 70 and so on. This bell-shaped curve is produced by careful design, and if there is any skewing of the curve it is a design fault. This is why it is important to look in the test manual to judge how carefully it was designed. The tables of norms in the manual enable raw scores on a test to be converted into standardised scores for the ages covered by the test. The production of a near-perfect, bell-shaped distribution in the design of a test is achieved by deliberately spreading children out through adjusting the level of difficulty of the items.

Sometimes tests are scored in percentiles. This indicates the relation between the child taking the test and those on which the test was standardised. Thus, a percentile score of 62 indicates that the child has performed at a higher level than 61 per cent of the population. Note, however, that the 'population' here is really the sample on which the test was standardised. Once again it is the care taken over the design of the test and the sampling for standardisation which matters.

Constructed at What Date?

Many of the most widely used reading tests are very old. Their popularity is often the result of the short time they take to use and the apparent simplicity of their construction. But there are dangers in an ageing test as it may never have been properly standardised. Tests rightly become popular because they are a handy aid to the judgement of the teacher. But they yield a score, usually a reading age, which can be taken as the basis of important decisions about children. Thus, the Schonell tests were published in 1942, and cover a wide age-range from 5 to 16.8, yielding a reading score. They were mostly standardised in the 1950s, although their continued use has resulted in later standardisation in the 1970s. Such re-standardisations are a help in bringing norms up to date, but they can be confusing. Scores have a tolerance built into them of plus or minus a few per cent. Thus, a score of 96 may really mean 94.5 to 97.5; but the re-standardisation may raise the score to 97. That will also have a tolerance, and may cover 95 to 99. Standards seem to have risen over the period since the original standardisation, but it would be difficult to be confident that a score of

97 on the second test was actually better than a score of 96 on the first.

Most of the popular tests in use were published in the 1960s or 1970s. Words can become redundant; norms can get out of date; the theories behind the tests can change. Above all, the schooling which tests sample can change. A reading age passed on to all secondary schools in a selective school system may have been useful once it had played its part in the selection. But it was likely that little use was made of this data; most secondary schools test on intake if they want reading scores. But what is often needed in comprehensive schools is information that will enable grouping to occur, and to sort out those children who will not be able to cope with the textbooks in use. In 1978 the Inner London Education Authority (ILEA) was asked by its Central Consultative Committee of Headmasters and Headmistresses to design its own *London Reading Test* (NFER, 1978) to be taken in the primary schools to indicate which children might need remedial teaching when they reached the secondary schools. The test was designed to pass on as much information on the level of attainment and the pattern of abilities as possible by using three passages linked to the textbooks most commonly used in the secondary schools. The test was constructed with the multi-cultural school population of London in mind. This information about the ability to benefit from secondary schooling without remedial help is of immediate use to teachers, yet no test existed that would do the job, or was suitable for such a population yet possessing up-to-date national norms. In most cases teachers have to use what is available, and it can be redundant.

How do You Choose a Test?

Teachers in junior or middle schools can usually find a test that fits their approaches to reading or to the curriculum. It is doubtful that any group test is worth using for the under-sevens. Here the informal methods described in Chapter 5 are as useful. Once the manual is read, the date and scoring arrangements checked, and it seems to fit the course organised by the teachers, it seems plain sailing. However, if tests are to be used for important decisions about transfer, or grouping, or monitoring standards, or screening for children who need help, advice needs to be taken. Most LEAs have specialist advisors or centres that can help. The NFER will also give advice.

The first decision is whether a group or individual test is required.

Usually teachers use group tests for assessing attainment, but tests such as the Neale Analysis of Reading Ability or the Standard Reading Tests of Daniels and Diack are used for more detailed diagnosis. But as tests tend to be used to provide a framework for the teacher to bring her own skill to bear to detect where the weaknesses lie, and because individual tests take time to administer, the group test is usually sufficient until more detailed diagnosis is required.

The second step is to read the manual to see if the test is for the right age-group, how it is to be administered, and what information it will yield. Very often the manual has been lost, or the often strict conditions for testing are impossible, or the teacher decides to skip some apparently pedantic instruction. Yet manuals that have not full details of administration are suspect, and minor deviations from instructions can bias the results. Here, for example, is a quote from the manual of the NFER Verbal Test EF (Wood and Land, 1971). 'No deviation, however slight, should be made from the oral instructions, since *any* alteration may have the effect of making the test easier or more difficult than the form for which standardised scores were obtained' (italics as in the manual). Two practical points remain: having decided the test is right and the cost not prohibitive, it is best to ensure that delivery can be obtained in time.

How Can Tests Best be Administered?

Test manuals usually give full instructions about administration, but with young children there are a few snags in following precise procedures. Instructions may not be understood. An upper limit of 20 in a group to be tested is wise, in case children need help. The usual instruction that children need two pencils is wise, because one of them distressed with one broken and no replacement can disturb the whole context. Ensure that there is relative peace and quiet, and no chance of someone rushing in to get three children out for a medical. Choose a classroom which is familiar. Above all, remember that the test is standardised, and this applies to its administration, as it does to its marking. They are tricky things even when instructions are followed. With liberties they can mislead.

How Can You Get as Much as Possible Out of Testing?

Assuming that the test has been administered correctly, a lot of information can be extracted even from an uncomplicated group test. First, it is wise to look at the distribution of scores for the group. If they are stacked up well below or well above the mean, the test was not appropriate for the ability of the children, even though the age-range may have been carefully chosen. Thus, inner-city children tend to score below the national average, and a test may prove too difficult for a majority. Alternatively, a very bright group may not be stretched and may stack up at the top. The consequences of this can be conceived by thinking of the absurd situation where a class of geniuses completed all the test items correctly. The test yields the very important information that the children are performing above, below, or at the level of the group on which the test was standardised, but the bunching at the ceiling or at the floor of the test scores reduces its power to discriminate between the children tested. There would be no spread, no bell-shaped curve and the real score might have been much higher than that indicated had the ceiling been higher.

The second check is to look at those individual cases where there is a discrepancy between test score and teacher assessment. If there are many of these, either the teacher or the test is in error. It is most likely that the teacher has not appreciated the purpose for which the test was designed, or is not for some reason on the same wavelength as the test designers. If it remains a mystery another test could be used. Tests are not infallible, but teachers can be mistaken, as it is difficult to establish norms for comparing standards inside a classroom with those outside.

Having checked the overall results, the teacher can look at the range of scores to establish the reading material that is needed for the spread of abilities in the group. This should include material below and above the ages indicated by the test, in order to stretch children and give them practice on materials they can deal with easily. The results should help the teacher plan the materials for future use.

Finally, the scores of individual children can be scanned to see where help is needed. Group tests such as the Edinburgh Reading Test for 10.0 to 12.60 ages test reading for facts, comprehension of sequences, retention of main ideas, comprehension of point of view and vocabulary. The profile produced from these five sub-tests is sophisticated and can yield very useful information, although it takes almost 2 hours to administer. A test such as the Gates-MacGinitie *Reading*

Tests, Primary Form 1 (British Edition, NFER, 1972) is especially useful in giving more information on those below, compared with those above 100 for pupils around age 7. As the two tests take only 15 and 25 minutes to complete they may be a more cost-effective way of obtaining information for bringing support to those falling behind than a test taking much more time.

Published Diagnostic Tests, Checklists and Inventories

Conventional norm-referenced tests compare one child with large groups of other children on overall performance. But what is more useful is often data on what has been achieved. When this point is reached, where use in the classroom is in focus, tests for assessment take second place to tests, checklists and inventories which help the teacher to help the children. If assessment is an inseparable part of teaching, it is through diagnosis, however tentative, that the link is made. In the second part of this chapter published diagnostic instruments will be described, but their use is discussed later alongside teacher-made instruments and routine teaching, because in practice teachers use all sources pragmatically. If they prove useful they will be used.

Most published tests are norm-referenced, suitable for assessing relative attainments, but not for identifying, describing, diagnosing and taking remedial action. However, there has been an increasing interest in publishing schemes to help teachers, particularly in helping children to read. These range from simple checklists to expensive structured tests. They range from screening young children so that those 'at risk' can be identified and helped, to checkpoints through which children across primary school ages can be guided. Many of these instruments have been carefully designed and validated. However, it is safest to see all of them as guides, not blueprints, aids to help teachers make decisions rather than independent indicators.

The amount of commercially published diagnostic material may be small, but it is supplemented by a large amount of material produced by LEAs. Again, a lot of this activity is to help teachers over early reading, and it has the advantage of the support of local advisors or inspectors, and of teachers' centres. Frequently such material has been produced by groups of teachers and advisors. This not only increases its relevance to local schools, but increases the chance that it will be revised as the organisation and curriculum of schools change. Finally, it tends to be cheap, and removes from teachers the temptation to break the law by duplicating copyright published material.

Screening Tests

Assessment is often seen as serving three purposes for the teacher: measuring attainment, identifying strengths and weaknesses, and indicating progress or deterioration. But assessment is also one way by which injustice can be avoided in education. If identifiable groups persistently attain at a low level and eventually leave school for unemployment, while other similarly identifiable groups move to higher education and promising jobs, then any technique that promises the early identification of strengths and weaknesses also offers the chance of doing something early enough in school careers to have an effect. This is the underlying attraction of screening, using assessment to identify those 'at risk'.

The parallel with medical screening is obvious. It is now possible to carry out checks early in a child's life to ensure that action can be taken to avoid harmful conditions developing later. Screening before birth is also possible to detect foetal conditions that require special action. The benefits in reducing human misery by a simple technique, such as a cervical smear for detecting possible cancer of the womb, are so great that an equivalent identification in early schooling would be an enormous boost to those liable to fall behind through a teacher's failure to notice that essential early steps had not been mastered.

Many attempts have been made to develop effective screening, usually in the infant schools. One well-documented scheme was introduced into all infant schools in Croydon in 1972 (Bullock Report, 1975). At the same time experiments were starting in the North-East, based on the University of Durham (Marshall and Wolfendale, 1977), ILEA (Hawkins, 1973), Somerset and other LEAs. The *Thackray Reading-Readiness Profiles* (1973) and other reading-readiness tests were published at this time. The Spooncer *Group Reading Assessment* (1964) was used in Waltham Forest, while others used Daniels and Diack (1958) or Young (1968). Most concentrated on early reading.

The Croydon scheme was typical in providing a package consisting of an observation checklist on children's development, the Neale *Analysis of Reading Ability* for use with infants, and the Young *Group Reading Test* for follow-up when children were in the first term of the second year in the junior schools. The ILEA Scheme was also based on a checklist to direct teacher observations. The scheme developed at the University of Durham was based on a criterion-referenced test to identify between 6 and 15 per cent of 'at risk' children of 6½ to 7½ years. The *Somerset Developmental Checklist* was designed to identify 'at risk' children of 5 years. This rush of activity at the start of the 1970s has not resulted in sustained systematic screening, and evaluations have been cautious. Nevertheless, LEAs make extensive use of screening tests, and the 1981 Special Education Act requires them to identify children with special needs. But diagnostic tests and screening profiles do not uncover why a child is failing. The problems are liable to be multiple, and many will lie outside the school. At any one time different combinations of factors may be influential, but as long as the test or screener is not seen as litmus paper having an inherently consistent quality, it can serve as a useful guide for teacher observations. But those observations, and the actions that follow, have to be sustained, not a one-off testing or recording with a label attached predicting future performance.

The Aston Index and The Aston Portfolio

The most sophisticated British screening programme was developed across the early 1970s at the University of Aston (Newton and Thomson, 1976). This programme has been developed for use by teachers, and the different parts are designed to identify those children likely to have difficulty in learning to read and to diagnose failures in older children. The *Index* is based on a theory of the written-language system, and the capacities required of a child in mastering it.

The *Index* contains checks on background factors such as physical condition, birth history and neurological factors, social background, the emotional climate of the home and the spoken language used. These background factors are checked, and only if the adverse conditions are not present is it assumed that some other factors are responsible for the difficulties identified. If the adverse conditions are present, an oral-language programme is recommended before attempting to introduce the child to the written language. Many of the factors in the *Index* require teachers to exercise psychological and sociological judgement of a very intimate nature.

The package for the systematic observation and assessment of the child consists of previously published and specially developed tests. Vocabulary, intelligence, picture recognition, copying, reading, spelling, visual sequential memory (pictorial and symbolic), auditory sequential memory, sound blending and discrimination, laterality and grapho-motor skills are included. The teacher can use the *Index* to produce a profile on a child, and this can point to remedial exercises or the need for further assessment. The exercises look interesting for the child, and the *Index* is attractively packaged. Thomson (1979), one of the designers of the *Index*, claims that the tests differentiate between good and poor readers and were correlated with further reading and spelling attainment. Thus, it is claimed that the *Index* is tapping underlying skills and can identify children 'at risk'. Furthermore, Thomson maintains that this classroom instrument for teachers is meaningful because it draws on the clinical experience of psychologists in helping children with reading difficulties. All children can be screened, and those 'at risk' detected.

The *Aston Portfolio* is a follow-up for teachers from *The Aston Index*, but can be used as a self-contained package. It consists of some 60 cards and requires no special apparatus. There are checklists of basic skills for reading, spelling and writing. These are designed to help teachers to identify what has gone wrong in the learning of these skills, and covers difficulties over reading, spelling, handwriting, comprehension and expression. This diagnostic section of the portfolio requires no special training to use.

The remaining cards present activities to help children over the difficulties detected through using the checklists. This 'tips for teachers' section contains about 500 suggestions to help with the problems identified. Most of them are in frequent use in primary school class-rooms as teachers have developed simple ways of helping children, but here they are collected together and related not only to the checklists for identifying problems, but to the tests that make up *The Aston Index*.

The *Aston Index* and *Portfolio* cover ground that is usually the preserve of experts, and there will be objections to packages that can be used without training by classroom teachers. But the diagnosis and remedial action cannot be left to experts, and are the continual practice of all teachers as they try to help children learn. Just as this book tries to extend professional practice in evaluation, so the work of the Language Development Unit at the University of Aston tries to help teachers in activities which have to be a central part of their work.

Diagnostic Assessment in Mathematics

Just as in the teaching of reading, so there are a large number of tests, inventories and checklists to help teachers assess individual performance in mathematics. These again range from modest instruments developed by LEAs, to structured packages and texts forming part of elaborate courses.

Many LEAs developed mathematics schemes in primary and middle schools to help overcome the shortage of specialist teachers, or to help in transfer from primary to secondary school. Many of these help teachers to detect where pupil strengths and weaknesses lie. Thus, Clwyd have produced an infant mathematics project tweely titled 'Mousematics'. It enables teachers to use flexible combinations of workbooks, number books and workcards. Teachers' notes give ideas on activities, preparation for work, books, charts, pictures and games that are suitable at each stage, and names of commercial firms who publish some of them. The most striking aspect of this package is a comprehensive, ingenious record card on which a lot of information can be recorded in little space. This has dates on which units were started and completed. The child works through the units and the teacher records progress by filling in boxes. For example, working through concepts is recorded in the same box by using one diagonal line for concept 'introduced', a further diagonal to produce a cross for 'can apply concept', and a vertical line through the cross for 'concept fully understood.' The scheme is not directly diagnostic, but teachers are helped by the recording of data on which diagnosis can be based.

A typical example of a directly diagnostic LEA mathematics assessment was produced in the Educational Development Centre of Birmingham Education Department in 1975 (Neal, 1975). The teachers looking at assessment found suitable reading and verbal reasoning tests, but no commercially produced instrument for mathematics. It was decided to produce a diagnostic assessment instrument. This consists of two papers covering basic number bonds and basic number skills, along with a third paper for testing concepts and problem solving. The test items are designed to give receiving secondary schools the scores of each child on the tests. The diagnosis is left to the secondary teachers looking through the answers to the three papers, providing a straightforward way of seeing where strengths and weaknesses lie.

Many assessing and recording arrangements are built into published mathematics schemes. For example, the Nuffield Mathematics Project (Nuffield Foundation, 1972), designed for children aged 5 to 13, contained check-up guides. These were prepared by a team from the Institut des Sciences de l'Education in Geneva where Piaget was working. These check-ups were designed to replace testing in a project built on individual discovery. They consist of suggested activities and ways in which teachers can observe individual children engaged in these, to gauge how well children are understanding.Typical replies to questions and typical actions are described illustrating the level reached by the child. There is no norm-referencing or straightforward assessment in these check-ups. They are designed for individualised work. They are based on a clear theory of mathematical development.

ILEA, Primary School Mathematics Checkpoints

The ILEA published curriculum guidelines in mathematics in 1976, and *Checkpoints* two years later (ILEA, 1978). These checkpoints are items describing something which a child can do, understands, or knows. These are used to build up a record of specific achievements and to serve as a diagnostic tool for teachers receiving a child or looking for precise points of difficulty. The checkpoints are not a replacement for teacher observations for diagnostic purposes, but a way of encouraging teachers to focus on important points to ensure that a base of ideas, skills and knowledge is built.

The four strands of the curriculum guidelines in mathematics, sets, numbers, measures and geometry, are covered by the checkpoints. Items are matched for age, (A) being 'usually found in nursery/infant school', (B) being 'usually found in last infant or first junior school', and (C) 'usually found in upper junior school'. Here, for example, is the checkpoint for weight, with the accompanying notes to help teachers set up the check.

CHECKPOINT	NOTES
CONSERVATION Knows that if an object is deformed it is just as heavy as before. CONCEPT A	The deformation may be done by splitting up or changing the shape or both. Modelling clay is useful here.
COMPARISON Can tell which is the heavier and which the lighter of two objects by: • holding one in each hand on a string. • putting them in the pans of a balance. • suspending them in turn on a spring or elastic. CONCEPT A	Fine differences are not expected at this stage. Judging just by holding can be deceptive due to 'spreading the load'. Hence the use of a string for holding. Balancing and suspension lead to the use of instruments for weighing.

CHECKPOINT

NON-STANDARD UNITS Can compare the weights of objects by balancing them against small non-standard units.
SKILL B

ORDER OF WEIGHT & SIZE Knows that the order of size (volume) and the order of weight of a set of objects is not necessarily the same.
CONCEPT B

STANDARD UNITS Can estimate, measure and record weight using suitable standard units and a range of weighing instruments.
SKILL C

PRACTICAL PROBLEMS Can carry out practical activities which need calculation with weights.
APPLICATION C

WRITTEN PROBLEMS Can solve written problems about weight.
APPLICATION C

KNOWLEDGE OF UNITS Knows common units of weight and their interrelationships.
KNOWLEDGE OF FACTS C

Source: ILEA, 1978, p. 17.

NOTES

Units such as beads which all weigh the same are useful as are identical cubes, metal discs etc. Items with variable weights themselves, for example conkers, fir-cones and shells, are useful only for introducing discussion about the need for uniform items.

The objects should include small metal ones and much larger wooden or plastic ones.

Units would include grams and kilograms. Several types of instrument such as beam balances, extending spring and compressed spring machines should be used.

This will involve combining measures in order to obtain a final answer. For example, finding the weight of liquid which can be held in a certain container.

Children need to understand the problem, decide which calculations to do, and perform them correctly by any method.

Once again, the advantage of this LEA-based development is that it has the support of advisors, teachers' centres, centralised production of learning materials and of the many teachers involved in developing the scheme. Teachers are encouraged to develop their own lists and observational skills as they go about everyday work in the classroom. Many will have gained the experience to do this in the working parties and pilot studies, and in designing the scheme. The booklet is supported by cards describing ways of finding out whether a child has mastered a particular checkpoint. These are produced by the ILEA Learning Materials Service. The guidelines were produced under the direction of the ILEA inspectorate.

A recurring theme in this discussion of a selection of published diagnostic aids for teachers has been that success depends on the active involvement of teachers in assessment. The checklists and tests can guide that involvement, but not replace it. Indeed, the danger of published diagnostic material is that it could discourage the exercise of professional judgement. If a test really pinpointed the time when a child was ready to read, or had mastered place value with two digits, the teacher could relax and depend on the instrument. In practice, readiness, mastery, learning difficulties and low attainment each have multiple causes which change over time. Having an instrument available helps the teacher move into the situation to help the child. It provides the questions, the activities, the possible problems. It sets up the diagnostic situation, and draws on available evidence to suggest hypotheses, hunches about remedial action. Another advantage of the locally produced instrument is that being developed with teachers, it is likely to use teachers' skills with the instrument and present the diagnostic materials in understandable form. This is likely to outweigh the theoretical sophistication and longer-term research behind the best of commercially published diagnostic instruments.

RECORDING PUPIL PROGRESS

There is necessary caution about records in schools. The time devoted to completing them is rarely matched by the time spent consulting them. As with evaluation generally, records are means not ends, and clarification of 'who needs what information' can avoid a lot of wasted effort. In practice the many purposes served are often best served by a number of specialist records. When those purposes are related to improving pupil learning the need for parsimony increases. Teachers remember hundreds of bits of information about children and about their curriculum. Some has to be recorded because it is too important to risk forgetting; some needs to be written down so that it can be passed on. But it has to be remembered that records are completed by teachers who are likely to know all about a child, and interpreted later by those who do not. The questions about reliability and validity asked in Chapter 1 are still important.

In any school there will be many different records. Most serve the bureaucratic aspects of the school. These include returns to the DES or the LEA, reports to governors, attendance registers, the headteacher's logbook, health records and the punishment book. In addition there will be records related to teaching and learning, including personal records on pupils, transfer records, and possibly teachers' mark books.

Most of these records are needed to run the school efficiently and to answer requests for information on children from the LEA or the Education Welfare Officer, or the Education Psychologist and so on. The education service is big and necessarily bureaucratic. Routines to help individual cases are achieved through the management of information in the DES, LEA, in schools and in classrooms. Organisations need basic information on file so that it is not necessary to collect it afresh every time it is required. Teachers need it to give coherence to the sequence of learning, and to give all children a fair chance to benefit. But information is explosive stuff. I may think it useful for schools and LEAs to have ethnic and social class data on their children because it can be used to ensure that identifiable groups are gaining from education; but others may object that the collection of such personal data cannot be justified on ethical grounds. We are in the world not only of improving practice, but of reconciling conflicting views. There is much concern about the content of records on children, and the trend to open records has been rapid (Hodges, 1981).

The emphasis on information rather than record cards is useful. There is a practical danger in pressure to record: means and ends tend to get mixed up. Records are always means to ends, not something that should exist in their own right. The perfect record system may be both exhausting to collect and too sophisticated to use. The Schools Council research into *Record Keeping in the Primary School* from 1976 to 1978 (Clift, Weiner and Wilson, 1981) confirmed that teachers see a wide variety of purposes for keeping records. Indeed, such a variety that it was seen as counter-productive. Much effort went into the records but they were often unread by those for whom they were written because they did not seem relevant.

What Goes Into School Records?

The conclusion from the Schools Council research on record keeping (Clift, Weiner and Wilson, 1981) was that no single record is going to suit all schools, not only because staff respond to local situations and work out their own curriculum, but because records that were thorough and used with enthusiasm in the research were those that served the way teaching was organised in the school. The successful records were the last stage in the process of teaching, not the first. The dog was wagging the tail! Where record systems were set up first and decisions about teaching followed, the records were likely to be pushed aside. The successful records were recently designed because as teaching changes records have to change, if they are not to become redundant. Finally, these successful records were the product of collaboration between all the teachers in the schools. If this was not the case the records would not be likely to fit the teaching. This conclusion points to important aspects of content, design and organisation that can guide useful record construction.

The Basic School Record

A headteacher or member of staff often has to obtain information on a child quickly. At other times returns have to be made to the LEA. The Education Act of 1980 requires schools to publish basic information. A central file is necessary to save work. Here is a typical basic record:

SURNAME	FORENAMES	DATE OF BIRTH day/month/year
Boy or Girl		
Home Address	Family Doctor	Religion
Daytime Contacts:	Tel No.	First Language
Father/Legal Guardian	Schools Previously Attended	
Mother		
Responsible Adult		

Obviously such basic information would have to be supplemented by any information important for the child's wellbeing, whether medical, academic or social. In the Schools Council study (Clift, Weiner and Wilson, 1981, pp. 145-8), LEAs included the following categories on transfer cards in over 75 per cent of cases:

Name	Parent's or guardian's name
Date of birth	Name of school(s) previously attended with dates
Home address	Comments on attainments

The range in the number of categories included on record cards stretched from 70 to 10. Only a third of record cards had any notes of guidance and use. Many were designed fifteen to twenty years ago. To the 163 teachers used in this research to assess what information was essential, the top twenty categories were, in descending order, date of birth, surname, forenames, home address, health or physical factors of importance, person to contact in case of emergency, telephone number in case of emergency, health handicaps that could affect progress in school, name of school attended at present, hearing loss, need for glasses, sex of child, home telephone number, learning difficulties, results of referrals to other agencies, speech defects, referrals to child/educational psychologist with dates, nature of any remedial treatment. The information on attainments was concentrated on the basic skills. Language and reading development were given priority, followed by mathematics. Few primary schools recorded development of study skills, science or other curriculum areas. A variety of norm and criterion-referenced assessments were used, based on tests, checklists and structured comments by teachers. In many cases records were completed using LEA guidelines and checklists.

Recording Pupil Progress

A line has to be drawn between the mass of remembered evaluations of pupils and those that are recorded. Furthermore, a decision has to be made about the information that is to go on to a school record rather than to a record held by the teacher. A basis for selection is to remember that recorded information should be both reliable and valid, and clearly referenced to some norm, criterion or previous performance. The earlier recommendation to restrict formal assessment so that when decisions are based on it they are not doing a possible injustice, still holds. It is best to limit recorded information, but to ensure that it has the characteristics of good assessment.

This minimal recording can be supplemented in three important ways. First, the pupils can keep their own records and evaluate their own work. This ability to self-assess is an important if neglected study skill. Pupils need to be taught to judge their own efforts, and keeping records of their progress is one aid to acquiring this ability. This skill can be started early. For example, The Schools Council *Initial Literacy Materials* (Thompson, Schaub and Mackay, 1968) recommended that children learning reading should accumulate words that they can read in a word folder of their own. They use these words in collaboration with other children to form sentences. Eventually the words in the folder will not be used because the child has become confident in the words accumulated. It is recommended that instead of using the common method of recording pupil progress by noting the pages and books that the child has covered, teachers should record the books read and use the children's folders to record the progress of word recognition through the number of words 'in the bag'.

Foster (1971) has recommended that children should not only record their progress, but evaluate their efforts, their contribution to group work, and summarise the work done during the week. In addition, he suggests that the pupil's record should be checked every week, and the teacher should organise regular meetings with pupils where the self-record will be discussed. Similarly, Davies, in a first school, involved children when they were individually tested for language development (Davies, 1980). The marking was carried out with the child so that errors could be discussed. The score sheet of the previous test was looked at together to see where there had been improvement. The children then worked out a programme for development with the head-teacher who was doing the testing. The children were invited to make a comment to be recorded on the score sheet. This development suggests that even young children can help contribute to records. This is beneficial to the child and good preparation for taking similar responsibilities later on in secondary school (Stansbury, 1979).

The second way of minimising the work of recording is to collect together pupils' work into a file as recommended in the Bullock Report (DES, 1975, para. 14.11). In *Primary Education in England* (DES, 1978) Her Majesty's Inspectors (HMI) found that 43 per cent of teachers reported using a folder of sample work to assess children on arrival to a new class. In practice such a folder might be far less misleading than a lot of data that comes through on record cards. It can also be interpreted by the receiving teacher. Interpretation is often difficult when all that is received is a norm or criterion-referenced assessment, where the assumptions built in by the compiling teacher or teachers, particularly in setting criteria, are unknown to the recipient.

The third way in which teachers can save on the amount they record while concentrating on its quality, is to substitute case conferences for record cards. It is the practice in social-work agencies for staff to discuss their cases together. This not only shares information on clients in case there is turnover of staff, but brings together different interpretations and suggestions for help. There is even more reward for this case-conference approach in the school where the same child may be in contact with many teachers. This is a favoured approach to the monitoring and reviewing of pupil progress in the East Sussex Accountability Project (Becher, Eraut and Knight, 1981). They recommend periodic dicsussions about individual pupils rather than attempting to produce bigger and better records. They point out that discussion with another teacher does not require any additional documentation. However, the East Sussex research, while critical of record keeping, goes no further than recommending regular discussions of pupils in a class with another teacher. But regular discussions can also be casual. If discussion were to replace records they would have to be organised, and arrangements for calling in the headteacher and for documenting and passing on important information would need to be agreed in advance. The advantages of a case conference approach in sharing information among teachers and bringing more knowledge to bear are obvious. The ideal combination would be a basic record-keeping system and regular case conferences with important conclusions recorded.

Where a member of staff took a particular interest in pastoral care, that teacher could act as a consultant. The headteacher would be called in where tricky cases were identified.

Profiling and Criterion-referenced Records

One of the spin-offs from taking assessment seriously is that it can help dispel the notion that a single mathematics or language or science score can sum up mathematical or some other attainment. One benefit from the APU's sophisticated testing is that the curriculum areas covered are not arbitrarily summarised by a single average that conceals the wide range of attributes that make up the areas of the school curriculum. In the effort to use assessment not only to monitor and inform, but to help teachers and pupils, profiles have become popular. If the important subject areas could be broken down into concepts, knowledge, skills and so on that could then be assessed, it would be possible to show the strengths and weaknesses of individual pupils in sufficient detail for action to be taken to help.

Here is a typical profile for science in the junior school:

Knowledge of science	Very Good	Good	Fair	Poor	Very Poor
Recall of facts					
Understanding					
Scientific skills					
Following instructions					
Collecting information					
Handling apparatus					
Observations					
Measurement and recording					
Evaluating evidence					
Applying evidence					

In Chapter 2 such checklists were discussed as guides for helping teachers to help children. Now the issue is their use as records to be stored, retrieved and distributed. The checklist above is unquestionably of more use than a single grade for science. It not only breaks the subject down, but gives the reader some idea of the way science is organised in the school, what is valued by the teachers, and how pupils are coping. But what is likely to be its reliability and validity as defined in Chapter 1? Taking the former, would similar gradings be given by different teachers or by the same teacher on repeated gradings? The chances of high reliability are low. The reason is clear from the crudity of the five choices. Furthermore, many checklists rely on a tick or a cross only. Try to work out what 'Very Good' means in this context when ticked opposite 'Handling apparatus'. You immediately start to ask further questions. What is the distribution of ticks across the class? Many teachers will only use the positive end of the scale; others may grade to spread grades out. A second question follows about the skill itself. Now we have switched to looking at validity. What was involved in this handling of apparatus? Was it care in handling a lens, chemicals for testing the acidity of soil, or tape measures? Was it the care taken, the dexterity exercised or the following of instructions that was 'Very good'?

The final set of questions refer to the ways of completing the record. How standard were the procedures? Were all teachers completing it using similar prescribed methods, or were they left to do it their way? Were the categories and the grades designed through sufficient trial runs to ensure that they would give a known spread, or is there a danger that they will cluster pupils at one end of the scale, or produce no consistent pattern? A standardised test has reliability because the instructions are precise and to be followed in all cases. Where this is not the case there is no guarantee that all have been assessed by the same means. Yet many checklists and profiles have scanty instructions, and the teacher is allowed to use a lot of discretion. This is fine for use in the classroom, but not for the transfer of important information.

These questions point to the major problem with checklists for records to be passed on to other teachers. To enable the reader to interpret confidently there has to be detailed and explicit information on specific, clearly defined characteristics. The list is liable to become endless to secure this degree of clarity. Profiling can result in record cards becoming booklets, and the question of cost-benefits becomes more serious. The Schools Council project on record keeping found that checklists were useful in focusing attention when observing children and in detailing the work covered. They were of less use in providing information about achievements, because the assumptions of those compiling and filling in the checklists were not known to those interpreting them 'in the dark'.

The second source of evidence on checklists comes from an evaluation of the Schools Council *Progress in Learning Science* project (Elliott, 1982). This project resulted in a very sophisticated system for recording scientific progress (Harlen, 1977). Elliott's evaluation was that teachers were likely not to use the method devised because of their 'practicality ethic'. It just would not be possible to give the priority needed to the time-consuming recording. This was not mere idleness: it was a practical evaluation of the realities of the situation faced.

The third piece of evidence comes from the ORACLE project based in the University of Leicester (Leith, 1981). Leith was trying to help teachers assess project work in the primary school. Forty-seven criteria were produced in collaboration with the teachers. Nine schools were selected to try out the criterion-referenced assessment sheet that was produced. Thirty teachers were involved in these schools. Yet while all were using projects in their teaching, none used the assessment sheets nor did any teachers systematically evaluate the work of the children. Yet this assessment was tailor-made for the task by the teachers involved. The message throughout this book has been that there is little point in designing sophisticated instruments that nobody will use. Yet the effort to consider profiling, criterion-referencing and so on may itself be an effective way of improving the quality of the judgemental evaluation that is used. The principle may be more important than the product.

The consequences of this gap between the need to extend profiles and checklists to give them meaning, and the pressure this builds up for teachers, can be cursory evaluation. The job is completed as quickly as possible, and in time is short-circuited or given up completely. This is not to devalue profiles or checklists; they are valuable teaching techniques for they alert teachers to important aspects and help them observe important, specific characteristics. They also provide detailed records. But they are not immediately meaningful to others. Much of a teacher's work is in rapid diagnosis of the learning difficulties faced by individual children or a class. Most of this comes through observations that may be unsystematic, but can be based on a lot of experience of similar cases. The tasks are analysed, the skills involved are known, and the individual circumstances are rapidly assessed to come to a course of action. A profile or checklist, or list of criteria, will help guide teachers to the important tasks and skills. Recording this information will help teachers to make it part of their professional armoury. Reliability and validity are open to challenge. But the thought that has gone into the profiles and checklists, often from working parties of teachers and advisors contributing all their available expertise, is consequently shared among teachers.

The consequences of introducing an elaborate scheme of profiling have been perceptively described by Frisby (1982). Having worked on an LEA scheme to produce profiles, he sees their use as changing the role of the teacher. Here is his description of this hidden agenda:

The difficulties of using the profile successfully relate to aspects of classroom organisation. At present I think most teachers see the profile as a not-so-simple substitute for the old record card. Not only is it fifty times as heavy, but it takes twenty times as long to fill it in, and the filling in has to be done every year, in some cases every term. Items have to be ticked off and comments written in, dated and initialled. Since there are over 100 attributes for each child (say 3,000 for each class) in the Junior profile alone, which have to be assessed, this is quite a handful for weary teachers trying to reconstruct the events of the past few months. The obvious answer is to be able to record significant events as they happen. But this cannot be done in classrooms given over to the predominant ideologies of individual attention or to class instruction. In the one, any attempt to sit back and observe and record for a few minutes leaves the teacher with a queue of eager individual attention seekers, and in the other an abdication from stage centre by the teacher will give the usurper on the front row his chance. So a profile system of this complexity can become an instrumental feature in changing the teacher's role, since it can lead to the adoption of classroom practices which encourage teachers to develop skills in participant observation, rather than didactic skills.

The problem of passing on information to guide other teachers is most acute at the transfer to secondary school. In many LEAs there are schemes for liaison between the teachers from the different stages. The LEA record is passed on, and contains not only basic information but often test scores, teachers' assessments and samples of the work of pupils. In the days of the '11 plus', test scores used in selection were often included on a record. These were usually in intelligence, an English and mathematics test. Some LEAs still use test programmes before transfer. One such battery consists of the NFER Non-verbal Test DH, the NFER Verbal Test D, the NFER English Progress Test D2 and the NFER Basic Mathematics Test DE. But tests are expensive, and their norm-referencing gives little information beyond that needed to select, group and balance intakes into schools.

The attempts to shift to criterion-referenced tests or profiles as transfer information have had limited success. The most ambitious has been conducted by the NFER in Hillingdon (Sumner and Bradley,

1977). The borough decided on six assessment exercises in English and twelve in mathematics. Plans to extend these exercises to other areas of the curricula were abandoned. Working parties had the technical help of the NFER, but the amount of work involved and the time taken in designing the profiles were underestimated. Further, the LEA simplified the English scheme when they came to use it. This attempt to produce good-quality profiles was supported with greater resources than are available to LEAs or teachers not involved in an experimental project. Yet it had only limited application.

Records for Maintaining Effective Teaching

Most teachers use a combination of written record of work planned, in progress and completed. But as with assessment, this is a minor part of the total recording. To sustain teaching there has to be running recording, short-term planning and a dependence on memory. While the days are past when all teachers had to keep a record of their teaching plans and progress, some recording is a safeguard against the casual. Students under training always have to plan their lessons and to evaluate their success. Usually a standard format is encouraged to ensure that it is done systematically. Once in teaching the detailed written lesson planning may be dropped. But the scheme of work is still important. It may be in published form such as the *Initial Literacy Project (Breakthrough)* (Schools Council, 1970), or be written by the teachers for their own school, or individual to a teacher. But some record is needed to ensure continuity.

The interest of inspectors and advisors in such schemes forms an important part of their evaluation of a school and of individual teachers. The need for schemes of work increases as teachers move away from a set syllabus and class teaching. This lies behind the interest of LEAs in producing guidelines for the basic, vehicle subjects. Any movement away from didactic teaching requires more, not less, planning, and much staff discussion about the curriculum is rightly centred on the adequacy of this course planning. The difficulty is to draw the line between the written scheme of work and the day-to-day implementation where the planning and evaluation is in the mind. Experienced teachers find that little has to be written down to help them achieve continuity, even when 30 children may be progressing through work at different speeds. But there is evidence that attention is unevenly divided between children and that some may be losing out because the teacher assumes that short-term planning can be carried in the head. Some regular evaluation of course planning by staff is a safeguard for the children.

This has been a depressing chapter for the technical optimist. But the chances of designing records that will be easy to complete, reliable, valid and informative to those who do not know either the teacher who completed them or the child to whom they refer, are low. Hence it is essential to give priority to the cost-benefit question. What combination of records will give the maximum information for the minimum of effort? At least some guidance can be extracted from the evidence available.

(1) The purposes of recording information have to be thought out in advance. Information of value to teachers in the classroom may be useless for other teachers, and the work required to make it useful may not be worth the effort.

(2) Records should contain basic information on the child, and details of any circumstances that should be known to teachers to ensure that an effective education can be organised.

(3) Information on attainments is difficult to interpret. It is often more useful and less work to include a sample of work by the pupil than poorly referenced, unstandardised test scores, checklists or profiles.

(4) The use of records is increased if all the teachers involved collaborate in the design.

(5) Comprehensive recording takes time, and is likely to affect the role of the teachers. Something may have to give, or teachers will make their own adjustments.

This is the point at which to conclude Part 1. Because evaluation serves many different purposes it is often a saving of time and effort to keep different purposes separate. Time needs to be given to designing tests for diagnosis, but not for keeping up the momentum of a question-and-answer session on learning to tell the time. Because evaluation should come out of the organisation of learning not the other way round, it is a useful way of defining priorities. In the learning of modern languages, graded tests and graded objectives go together. Checklists, inventories and profiles incorporate teachers' priorities. Here, for example, is a skill with its accompanying observations for the assessment of primary school social studies, taken from *Social Studies in the Primary School* (ILEA, 1980, p. 31). If evaluation is seen as part of the organisation of learning, the recording of such information is a reminder of the priorities established by the teachers.

SKILL
OBSERVATIONS

The organisation of information into hypotheses
• Often develops a hypothesis from the materials used when studying a particular topic.
• Realises that this is only a hypothesis and will need testing.
• Can test the hypothesis.
• Can re-think the hypothesis in the light of new evidence.

This is one of eight skills and accompanying observations in this profiling of social studies in the primary school. Each defines the emphasis in the course. The booklet is a definition of objectives and methods, and the assessment not only helps teachers to monitor the progress of children, but reinforces the objectives. Evaluation is concerned with diagnosis, guidance, grading, selection and prediction. But it is also concerned with underlining what is important in the curriculum, and for children to master.

The often different purposes served by assessment and recording account for the conclusion that it is often better to separate the various parts of evaluation and record keeping that serve different purposes. This is why it often turns out to be more informative and less work to pass on samples of children's work with some basic data, rather than designing sophisticated records and complicated assessments. It is not just that the work is there anyway; it is that the receiving teachers can then carry out their own assessment on their own assumptions. If objective evidence is required, an objective test might help. But once again, this might be left to the receiver to avoid re-testing, unless some agreement over the test to be used can be obtained in advance.

Thus we can end Part 1 with the often-heard complaint from teachers that there are opportunity costs to assessment and to record keeping. Something else has to be sacrificed. Many staffs do manage to carry out, as routine, procedures that others consider impossible. But there is a point where the most efficient staff will have to give something up. Choices have to be made. This is why the emphasis has been on assessment to support the effective organisation of learning and on recording to sustain it as children move through school. That suggests a criterion for deciding between priorities. Highest priority should be any activity that produces high benefits in learning for the lowest input of time and energy.

PART TWO

EVALUATING THE SCHOOLS

6 IN-SCHOOL OR SELF-EVALUATION

In the second half of this book the focus shifts from evaluating the work of pupils to the school itself. The concern is with organisation and management. It is with the way learning is organised. The selection of aspects of the school has been arbitrary. The staff of each school are liable to have their own list of priorities, whether arising from a considered appraisal of their management, or through some emergency that needs consideration and action.

At the heart of the evaluation of the school lie the same principles and procedures as outlined in Chapters 1 and 2. The questions to be asked are still about reliability and validity. The assessment can still be against norms, against criteria, or against previous performance. There is still the necessity for staff to see evaluation as an integral part of the way they run the school, just as this was central to the organisation of learning in the classroom. Just as discussion, planning and the exchange of views secured professional judgement to back up more conventional classroom assessments and the occasional objective test, so school evaluation is largely a matter of teachers honing up their impressions to increase their reliability and to cross-check them.

There is a similarity between self-evaluation and the evaluation of pupil performance, because both need to be selective. This is not only the result of pressure on the time of teachers. Parsimony ensures that all-embracing schemes for evaluation are not adopted without thought for the inevitability of superficiality. School evaluation, like that of pupils, can become an end in itself. Profligacy is wasteful whether it occurs in excessive testing, elaborate profiling, obese records or management by too many objectives. If too much is attempted it will be superficial, for teachers have priorities that promote evaluation when it promises to pay off in learning, whether through more effective classrooms or more effective school organisation.

The choice of school topics discussed was determined partly because they were important. The curriculum and organisational aspects such as public relations, staff development, records and internal communications are clearly central to the working of the school. But there is also a wealth of literature about curriculum evaluation. Similarly, there is a long tradition of evaluating experimentally. Both can be used for helping teachers to look systematically at specific developments in their work. There is also a new but useful literature on school self-evaluation that has been used to suggest ways of improving the more usual off-the-cuff impressions. But in every case the same principles apply as in the evaluation of pupils. Pupil and school evaluation are both examples of the search for valid and reliable information on human behaviour. The effort to find a way of exercising some control over judgement, while not destroying its validity by being too rigid, applies to teachers as they evaluate as it does to all social scientists.

There is a final and crucial similarity between the evaluation of pupils and of schools. The literature on both tends to present techniques that teachers may use if they fit their requirements. The approach here by contrast is to present ways of structuring everyday impressions and judgements. Just as the important aspect of the organisation of learning is that teachers carry the structure around in their heads as they go about their work, so evaluation is best developed as a model, a picture in the mind, that can guide action as it is planned.

Just as it is normal practice for teachers in the classroom to adjust their work through instantaneous evaluation of the responses of children, so it is becoming increasingly common for teachers to review the working of their school and to use their judgements as immediate feedback to alter their organisation. The light in the eyes of the children serves as a basis for speedy adjustments in teaching style and for quick curriculum development. Similarly, a snap judgement on the state of the buildings, or a scan of recent developments in the teaching of science, can serve to initiate action to tidy things up or change the way things are organised.

As with the evaluation of the work of children, the concern of this second half of the book is to encourage this important and useful impressionistic evaluation, and to convert it into a more thorough review programme. This can range from regular meetings to discuss the curriculum, the pastoral arrangements, attainments, co-operation with parents and so on, to systematic evaluation involving the setting of objectives and the establishment of criteria for determining achievements. The common aim is to keep priorities and procedures under continuing review. The advantage of structuring this is the same as for pupil evaluation. It builds in checks on personal impressions, and ensures that there is no great gap between what is believed to be happening and what is actually going on.

While internal review and evaluation are extensions of the everyday running of the school, the production of information for those outside the school is more sensitive. For example, in the East Sussex/University of Sussex project on accountability in middle schools (Becher, Eraut and Knight, 1981), the teachers accepted that they were morally accountable in their relations with pupils and with parents. They also accepted that they were professionally accountable for the curriculum and teaching methods they adopted. But they did not accept that they were contractually accountable to the LEA which employed them or to the governors of their school, or to parents. They did not feel bound to render an account of their actions.

The movement to self-evaluation by school staffs, whether on their own initiative or through the publication of an LEA scheme for their use, has been rapid. Late in 1980 Elliott found that out of 105 LEAs that responded to his enquiries, 69 had initiated discussions about self-evaluation in schools (Elliott, 1981). Twenty-one authorities had produced guidelines for primary schools and 17 for secondary schools. The movement has continued to flourish with other LEAs joining in since then, with the Open University producing a course on *Curriculum Evaluation and Assessment in Educational Institutions*, (Open University, 1982a) and the Schools Council making self-assessment part of one of its programmes of activities and funding a research programme in self-evaluation for primary and secondary schools under the title *GRIDS* (University of Bristol, 1982).

Most of the schemes published by LEAs follow the ILEA's *Keeping the School under Review* (ILEA, 1977) in asking questions to ensure that teachers are looking critically at their procedures and are monitoring the attainments of their children. The LEA-initiated schemes range from Oxfordshire, where it is planned that every school in the county will report every few years to school governors and to the schools sub-committee of the Education Committee, to many LEAs such as Birmingham or Solihull where self-assessment documents have been produced and offered to the schools but with no compulsion.

Steps to Self-evaluation

Most documents on self-evaluation produced by LEAs realistically stick to suggesting questions that staff can ask about important aspects of school organisation. Similarly, many school staffs have decided to review their work by producing lists of questions as an agenda. There is no doubt that it is useful for teachers to review their work in this way. But just as impressions of pupil performance have limited value, so have such judgements about the school. Once again, it seems more useful to follow the procedure in Chapter 2 and suggest ways of progressively improving impressionistic evaluation, than to recommend time-consuming and technically difficult methods.

The steps recommended for school evaluation are the same as those for pupil evaluation. Definition, selection, referencing, building into decision-making and improvement through practice remain ways of getting more valid and reliable judgements, and of using them more effectively. As before, any movement along this road is likely to be useful and the first steps are straightforward.

However, there are other advantages in approaching school self-evaluation in this way. First, accepting, adopting or producing lists of questions to guide internal review can be misleading. LEA documents have a hidden agenda, prescriptions among the descriptions. Questions define what is seen as appropriate organisation. Secondly, such lists of questions may also be alien to the style of any particular school; their definition and selection may be inappropriate. Thirdly, such lists rarely take account of the school as an organisation, yet evaluation is concerned with effectiveness, with causes of problems, reasons for successes and assumptions among different groups. Teachers have to ask 'why?' in order to find ways forward. The answers lie in the particular context of the school. Fourthly, the teachers most likely to review their work are just those who are most likely to be pressing on by themselves. They will have an idea of where they want to go and how to get there. Questions designed for a number of schools in an LEA document could deflect the efforts being made. Worse still, it is in just such schools that staff have a model of what makes the school tick that gives meaning to evaluation. Evaluation has to take account of context, or it can distort.

The five steps (a) to (e) that follow, incorporate progressive structuring as recommended for the evaluation of pupils. But in later chapters the concern is more often with deeper questions about how school organisation is seen in the minds of those doing the evaluation. Evaluation and improvement are not only matters of technique; they require judgements about how people work together, use resources and give of their best.

(a) Seeing the School as an Organisation
Getting a view of your part in an organisation is an essential first step to evaluating it. This is also an essential step in schools. The more staff stress that the school is small enough or intimate enough not to need any formal organisation or evaluation, the more need there

usually is for a detached look. Informality often means that processes are left unscrutinised. Yet someone is always probing. It may just be staffroom gossip. It may be over coffee before a meeting of governors. It may be among inspectors in county hall. It may be parents talking about their own or other people's children. Somewhere judgements are being made. Self-evaluation from inside the school can be an antidote to less informed judgements outside. Accounts of the running of the school can counter some of the more damaging rumours.

However, self-evaluation is also impossible without consideration of the school as an expensive organisation. A school that is organised as a hierarchy, with a headteacher who hands down instructions, and where staff are given detailed definitions of their roles, would find it very difficult to organise a bottom-up, 'democratic' self-evaluation. A school where information and decision-making were shared, and where teachers were left to establish their own routines would be unlikely to accept a top-down, 'mechanistic' form of assessment. Left to themselves a school staff are likely to arrange a style of self-evaluation that will fit their own organisation. An LEA-initiated exercise could jar against an organisation that incorporated contrasting principles. It might of course be very invigorating to have top-down assessment in a bottom-up organisation and vice versa. But it is no use ignoring the organisation within which the evaluation is to be introduced.

(b) Seeing Self-evaluation in the Management of the School
There is an assumption in this heading that schools should be managed. Even the most lackadaisical school staff and contented headteacher will have taken decisions about organisation and the allocation of scarce resources. But there is a temptation for teachers to assume that things are going well provided they are going smoothly (Becher, Eraut and Knight, 1981). Even a modest commitment to self-evaluation among staff means that management can be based on the information collected, and that strengths and weaknesses can be identified, reinforced or remedied.

Most of the models of evaluation assume that the school is a system in which the parts are interrelated, and that aims and teaching methods can be changed once information has been collected through evaluation. Much school self-evaluation is based on this systems model, with feedback as the key to continuous improvement. Here is the most popular model wherein evaluation feeds back to improve organisation and modify aims.

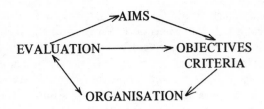

While aims are always held implicitly, their identification and definition can be time-consuming for staff. Furthermore, they may either be at a level of generality which makes them of little use in moving to examine means for their achievement, or they distract attention from more urgent areas where action needs to be taken. Hence an alternative model for placing self-evaluation into the management of the school is to keep the same feedback structure, but to select priorities through an initial review of current practices. Here is the model for the Schools Council activity based at the University of Bristol titled *Guidelines for Review and Institutional Development in Schools, (GRIDS)* (University of Bristol, 1982). This scheme for self-evaluation has six booklets, each containing steps for a review of priorities. Staff are guided through the processes of self-evaluation and the review of practices from Booklet 1 *Getting Started*, to Booklet 6 on *Feedback of the Outcomes*. The model for initial review is as follows:

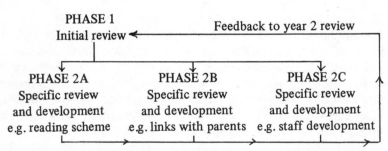

Here again we have the concept of continuous feedback from evaluation. Once the specific reviews have been completed there are booklets for acting on the review, evaluation of the development and on the way the outcomes of the exercise can be fed back into the running of the school.

There are objections to these systematic, feedback models. They assume that schools work with a synchronisation, an interrelation between teachers, headteacher, non-teaching staff, governors, parents, pupils, LEAs and so on that makes it useful to think of development as best achieved through securing a circulating flow of evaluative information. The reality is often more messy. Yet the model is important because it incorporates the prospect of improvement and of producing the information that makes this possible. Above all, the emphasis on feedback increases the chances that the evaluation will be used.

(c) Putting the Staff in the Picture

In early LEA documents on school self-evaluation there was no discussion of the perils facing the pioneer. Yet the first schools to publish a frank, hard-hitting account of wide-ranging performance would probably be empty of children in a period of falling rolls within a short period. Within such a school acrimony would be rife as strengths here were compared with weaknesses there. Later LEA documents acknowledged this political sensitivity. Here is the wise introduction to Stockport's self-evaluation scheme (Metropolitan Borough of Stockport, 1982, p. 4).

If self-evaluation is to be more than a hollow exercise, then it must take place in an atmosphere of trust. If the powerful have always been able to ask about the weak, the weak have always found the ways to deny them an answer. Self-evaluation at its best is a process in which individuals at all levels in an organisation are free to ask themselves and others about the work they are doing, and to respond as they will.

The unanticipated and potentially unpleasant consequences of published self-evaluations are enough reason for ensuring that teachers are fully informed of what is proposed. But teachers are also in the best position to identify aspects that should be given priority for evaluation. It is also necessary to establish the trust of the governors of the school. In early negotiations with professional associations in inner London after the introduction of *Keeping the School under Review* (ILEA, 1977), the teacher representatives pointed out that if there were a hundred questions, governors would want the hundred answers. Indeed, legally it would be difficult to deny them such information. Parents too would be most interested, and the 1980 Education Act has whetted the appetite for information. Internally and externally trust has to be established at the start.

(d) Anticipating the Production and Publication of a Report and its Audience
It is usually too late to consider the form of any report and its audience when the self-evaluation exercise has started. Just as an author decides on his chapter headings and then starts researching content, so self-evaluation needs to be guided by the form of report required. There are three aspects to consider. First, the use to be made of the information collected should be considered. If important decisions are needed, a heavier investment of time and energy will be justified than in the evaluation of a trivial issue. Evaluation of a proposal to integrate several subjects or to introduce vertical grouping should receive more attention than a report on the pros and cons of holding normal assembly for the whole school. It is also more profitable to concentrate on issues where action on the evidence collected is possible. There is little point concluding that extra staff are required when the priority is to avoid further redundancies.

The second consideration should be the time that can be made available. Planning can help. Some times of the year are busier than others in the school year, and the evaluation can be slotted into slacker periods. But staff will still have to find time. Casual meetings, attempts to use coffee or lunch breaks rarely work. The most satisfactory arrangements are for time-tabled time, or for regular sessions on evaluation after school or around the start or finish of terms. Most schools have busy periods to be avoided and others where the extra work is possible. The key is routine. Evaluation can be a 'nine-day damp squib' unless it is built into the routine running of the school. The focus may change, but the process of self-evaluation should become an accepted part of school management.

The third and most important consideration is to decide who is to get any report that is made. A confidential document is likely to contain very different material from one open to all. It is easiest to establish the trust of staff if self-evaluation is started as a modest way of sharing judgements between colleagues over the way homework is set and marked, or the teaching of study skills, or the use of pupil records and so on. Too early a move to evaluate sensitive issues could create problems that might jeopardise co-operation. For example, evaluating teaching performance needs very careful planning. Even if weak teachers should not be protected, their exposure would damage the rest of the staff, as the school will be judged as a whole by parents who cannot choose who takes their child. But children could also be harmed by open reporting of all evaluations by teachers. Most agendas have reserved items, for teachers have responsibilities towards children that require confidentiality. It is unfair to children to be known to be in receipt of free meals, in a school with a major delinquency problem, or in a withdrawal unit for the uncontrollable. It may be useful for teachers to know a child's reading age or intelligence quotient, but it is not something to make public.

(e) Setting About the Work

Once a decision has been made about the aspects to be evaluated, the teachers are in a similar situation to any evaluators. The same questions about reliability, validity and credibility apply. So do the technical steps that can ensure that even if the information collected is not completely objective, its shortcomings will be appreciated and taken into account. Because the same stages should be followed as in any research, including evaluation, the sequence of structuring in Chapter 2 still applies. By taking each of these stages, the evaluation can be conducted more systematically.

Stage 1: Definition of What is being Assessed. Once the choice has been made between trying to evaluate the performance of the school as a whole or of particular aspects, there is a need to define the area chosen. Once again, this is to convert the impressions and spot judgements about the school, or the curriculum, or staff development, or ways of assessing, into terms that will be clear to participating staff or to any external audience for any report.

Definition is needed for even the simplest form of evaluation. When a business prepares a balance sheet it is clear what is being assessed. Current and capital accounts are distinguished. The content of the resources used and the output sold or placed into stock, with the profit or loss made, are carefully defined and auditors confirm the figures. Teachers need nothing as elaborate as this, but they do need to ensure that their judgements about the extension of beginning reading skills, or the way potential truants are identified, or the way parents are kept informed, are about the same thing, and can be accumulated into a collective basis for action.

Stage 2: Selecting Key Aspects for Assessment. It may seem obvious that evaluation, because it is time-consuming, should be concentrated on important aspects of the work of the school. But it can become an end in itself. Being seen to be doing self-evaluation could easily become the equivalent of the late 1960s tendency to always be seen to be engaged in some sort of curriculum development, preferably a Schools Council project. It keeps advisors and HMI happy, impresses governors and is a useful answer when parents press for some change in procedures. Even irrelevant facts and figures can provide a defence against uninformed criticism. But useful evaluation depends on selecting key activities for scrutiny. Sometimes these will be problem areas, sometimes aspects affected by external changes, sometimes where a response is needed to a report or a changed LEA policy, but often because staff feel the need for a re-think. Staff development becomes crucial as replacements are not made due to economies. Falling rolls force a re-think of grouping practices and bring the possibility of vertical grouping into focus. The Warnock Report or a language-across-the-curriculum policy are typical reasons for the selection. Alternatively, as described earlier, the decision may be to look at the organisation of the school as a whole.

The importance of the area is the first basis for selection. The second is the chance of taking action on the evaluation. It should be aimed where the minimum investment of time and resources is likely to produce the maximum benefit. Staff can change internal organisation, curriculum, relations with parents, the form of assessment and teaching styles; they cannot easily change the nature of children, capitalism or the housing stock around the school. Many factors outside schools influence the attainments of children. It pays to raise sights every now and then and consider broader issues. But most improvements are modest and evaluations rarely come up with dramatic, radical recommendations based on sound data that can be implemented within the education service.

Earlier in this chapter, two models used in school self-evaluation were presented. These models typically start with the specification of aims. It is not easy to get agreement among school staff at this rather philosophical level, but a useful start is a list of existing aims. Here is the DES, *A Framework for the School Curriculum* list (DES, 1980a, p. 4)

(i)   to help pupils to develop lively, enquiring minds, the ability to question and argue rationally and to apply themselves to tasks, and physical skills;
(ii) to help pupils to acquire knowledge and skills relevant to adult life and employment in a fast-changing world;
(iii) to help pupils to use language and number effectively;
(iv) to instil respect for religious and moral values, and tolerance of other races, religions, and ways of life;

(v) to help pupils to understand the world in which they live, and the inter-dependence of individuals, groups and nations;
(vi) to help pupils to appreciate human achievements and aspirations.

It is possible to start with aims such as these and to set up specific objectives, standards or criteria that can be used to assess whether the aims have been achieved. The criteria will mostly involve professional judgement rather than testing, as with most criterion-referenced pupil evaluation. The advantage of such an approach is that teachers are given a framework within which to use their judgement. But it is unlikely that they will be unanimous either in that judgement or in the appropriateness of the criteria chosen.

The alternative to this holistic evaluation of the school is to be incremental, to evaluate one aspect before starting on the next. The selection can be from what Becher, Eraut and Knight (1981, pp. 79–81) describe as scanning or spotting activities, the former systematic, the latter incidental, but both part of the teacher's antennae for detecting potential problems. The advantage here is that a start can be made quickly on urgent problems. The snag is that the individual evaluations may remain separated and the school may be little affected. A model for binding them together is presented in Chapter 7.

Stage 3: Referencing the Evaluation. One perennial problem faced by more objectively minded teachers is that there is no easy reference against which the resources, or the organisation, or the successes and failures of a particular school can be compared. Evaluating internal processes is useful, but sooner or later you need to know how you are doing in relation to others. There are no universally agreed criteria for success, or ready-made tests. Standardised test results are justifiably judged inadequate or inappropriate by teachers when suggestions are made that they facilitate comparisons between schools. However, this lack of ready reference is a greater problem when looking for criteria for assessing performance than when assessing the way this is achieved. There is plenty of material now available from the DES, from LEAs, from the APU, from researchers and from individual teachers writing in journals such as *School Organisation*, for teachers to have a choice of comparative information on what others are doing. Processes can be improved even if the product has to be taken on trust.

There are four possible ways forward to references for school self-evaluation. First, many LEAs have solved the problem for schools by providing booklets on evaluation. Thus the Metropolitan Borough of

Stockport's *An Introduction to Self-evaluation* (1982), prepared by teachers and advisors, has separate booklets entitled *Classroom and Departmental Organisation, the Curriculum, Assessment and Student Evaluation, Management Structures, Decision-Making, Communication and Staff Development, Pastoral Structures* and *Social and Personal Education*. These are for the incrementally minded. But there is also a separate booklet on the in-school evaluation of the quality of the whole institution of the school. This booklet offers materials 'aimed at producing a catalytic effect which will encourage participants to stand back from their schools, in order to gain some kind of understanding of the total nature of their work' (Metropolitan Borough of Stockport, Education Division, 1982). Most LEA documents have sections on specific aspects of school organisation and questions on the school as a whole. Teachers wishing to start self-evaluation can use one of these documents as a menu whether 'à la carte' or 'table d'hôte'. But it always has to be remembered that the advisors and teachers who usually prepare the booklets were asking questions about the school in a form that suggests how it should be organised.

The second approach is to go for problem-solving or maintenance as a starter. Becher, Eraut and Knight (1981, pp. 22–6) see the former as short-term and specific, the latter as long-term monitoring to preserve and enhance the quality of organisation. The distinction is useful because of the need to build evaluation into the ongoing running of the school. Hence problem-solving has to be tied in with maintenance, or the staff will just be responding to occasional crises rather than improving the ongoing organisation. But either can be used to start self-evaluation, for the scanning and spotting that all teachers employ throw up ready-made issues for evaluation, and the changing environment of schools creates a continuing need for adjustments in routine.

The third approach is to refer to LEA policies and circulars, reports and surveys by HMI, APU results or to research evidence. There are two levels of issue raised by such external sources. At the most profound level there is over fifty years of evidence that identifiable groups of children have persistently performed below average. One valuable focus for self-evaluation is to look at the attainment of the children of unskilled or semi-skilled workers. More recently the evidence on the low attainment of blacks has produced another cause for concern. Others are the sex-typing of girls and the attainment of the least and most able. The other level at which official reports and research can be useful is in providing information on what is going on nationally. Surveys by HMI, reports by APU and surveys such as Bennett *et al.*

(1980) or Boydell (1981), can indicate how curriculum, or classrooms, or teaching styles, are organised in schools across the country. A research report such as *Extending Beginning Reading* (Southgate, Arnold and Johnson, 1981) can challenge the way most teachers organise the teaching of reading among the 7 to 9-year-olds, and lead to an evaluation of teachers concentrating on listening to individual children reading to them. Surveys and research are continually throwing up challenges to the way learning is organised. Any school wanting to start evaluation in a practical, useful way could benefit from the evidence from the ORACLE project (see, for example, Galton and Simon, 1980) which contains much challenging data on the way teaching is organised and the way children respond.

A modest example of the use of an external source has been reported by a primary school headmistress interested in the matching of children's abilities to the curriculum (Bruce, 1981). This had formed a substantial part of the HMI *Primary Education in England* (DES, 1978). Bruce organised evaluation in her primary school to check the match of curriculum to ability. This involved looking at standards of work and at the responsibilities of teachers. Checklists were produced to lead teachers. The assessment of match of ability to curriculum was organised using schedules reproduced in the appendix of the Primary Survey. Thus, the results could be compared with those reported by HMI.

The fourth approach is to refer to a theoretical model of school organisation or of the curriculum such as that in Chapter 7. This is the most ambitious approach. There is an example in the follow-up of the *Curriculum 11 to 16* 'Red Book' (DES, 1977) where 41 schools in five LEAs co-operated to review their curricula. This involved co-operation between local advisors, HMI and teachers in the schools, using the eight-fold categorisation of curricular areas in the 'Red Book' as a model. Many schools have found Skilbeck's situational analysis useful (Skilbeck, 1976) because it starts with an analysis of the context of the school. This is a high-risk approach. It can bring big gains if the staff can stick with it and work out their own principles and procedures in relation to the model chosen. But it can become academic and lead to little practical action.

Behind these four ways of obtaining comparisons is the tricky question 'How can we tell how well the school is performing?' As with pupil evaluation there are three ways forward. The first involves setting up standards against which the school will be evaluated. The second depends on comparisons against norms established outside the school. The third uses data accumulated over time. Normally evaluation will involve aspects of all three, and this evaluative data will accompany descriptions of the ways the school is organised in the aspects under consideration. Illuminative evaluation designed to produce a qualitative account became very popular, once the difficulties of establishing criteria, norms and indicators of performance were appreciated. It is very useful to obtain accounts of the way information is disseminated through the school, or how well informed parents are about the attainments of their children. It is a basis for evaluating the processes concerned. But if decisions are to be made to improve situations, there is going to be evaluation, and that requires some reference for the judgements, even if this is only to the professional criteria, norms or experience of the teachers involved.

(i) Criterion-referencing. Setting standards against which performance can be assessed is not easy. The sequence usually recommended is to agree on broad aims, to break these down into objectives, to set up standards or criteria or indicators of those objectives, to collect the necessary information, and then to place it against the standards to see if they have been attained and at what level. Examples are given in later chapters, where selected aspects are evaluated. This sequence is a useful guide for teachers but is rarely straightforward. But it has one major advantage. Thinking out the criteria is itself a means of reviewing priorities and ways of achieving them.

(ii) Norm-referencing. There are few national or local norms external to a school that can be used in evaluation. In theory any norm-referenced test could be used for this purpose. Schools often publish reading ages or scores against the national average of 100. With the variety of tests available yielding norms in reading, mathematics, study skills and so on, a range of comparisons should be possible. But this is deep and muddy water. A look at any APU report will show the problems. Instead of dots on a graph to mark a score, the APU give the dot with a line extending in the plus and minus direction to show the range within which the scores probably lie. A score of 110 can stretch to around 105 to 115. This is with very large samples, and when numbers are a year-group of fifty or less the latitude is wider. Other problems abound. The school might be unrepresentative of the group on which the test was constructed. Again, a look at APU reports will show the differences between metropolitan and non-metropolitan areas, north and south, girls and boys and so on. Furthermore, one or two absences can distort the averages, for absentees are often the weaker

pupils and their absence boosts the score. The exclusion of non-readers, or newcomers who speak no English is another problem. There are so many possible snags that the norms are a rough guide rather than a fixed marker.

It is of course still useful to use standardised tests. If year after year they yield consistent results compared with national norms, confidence in them is increased. There are also other comparisons that can be made from test scores. If the focus of evaluation is on the relative attainment of boys and girls, tests yield both. Many tests and APU reports, break down subject areas, so that a school could look at its performance in the various sub-sets of mathematics or of science or language. Some LEAs can also provude local norms through authority-wide test programmes.

It is, however, when a broader definition of norm is used that they become more useful to individual schools. The HMI survey of primary schools (DES, 1978), the reports from APU, research reports such as Bennett's study of open-planned schools for the Schools Council (Bennett *et al.*, 1980), contain descriptions and data on the way schools are organised, the way teachers operate and the way children respond. These are standards against which a school can compare its own operation. There is no better or worse here, but the comparisons can be the basis for informed judgements by the staff after examining the differences and their implications.

(iii) Self-referencing. Collecting data year after year can often result in storing the redundant. But there are two reasons for setting-up and graphing indicators so that trends can be examined. First, they may show progress or regress in selected and important areas. Secondly, they may reveal issues which need action. Scores on standardised tests graphed as time series year after year, for boys and girls, in reading and mathematics, for different age groups, for different social classes as indicated by parental occupation, for blacks and whites, can show up emergent or disappearing problems. They can promote action and show the effects of existing arrangements.

A typical example is absence obtained by register checks. Collecting figures on non-attendance may seem pointless, but when those absences are separated into different lengths, different days of the week, different terms, when the different excuses are classified, hunches about individuals and groups become profitable. A simple register check across a couple of terms in inner-London primary schools in the 1970s showed patterns of absence among juniors that suggested that action by Education Welfare Officers to check truancy among secondary school pupils may have been too late in many cases. The habit and the condonement came earlier. Furthermore, there were different patterns between different age groups. One of the few research findings to recur consistently is that time-on-task affects attainment. If more mathematics is taught, children are liable to learn more. But schools differ in the length of the school day, the length of term, whether setting homework or not, in the time allocated to academic work, while children have different rates of attendance and do homework set in different ways. Checking attendance can be a first step to the early identification of learning problems to come. Ensuring that work set is done, marked and fed back to children, that absence is followed up, and children helped to catch up when they return, is part of the evaluation of school organisation discussed in later chapters. Data collected, stored and retrieved provides another source for the teacher to decide on action on the basis of an examination of how things seem to have changed.

Stage 4: Building into Teaching and Learning. The flow diagram in Chapter 2 showing the feedback of information from evaluation into the organisation of learning is derived from models of the organisation as a system in which the parts have an organic relation to each other. The truth in this simplified model is that there is no point in evaluation unless it can be fed into improving the aspect being evaluated. This is most clear in reviewing the curriculum, or in evaluation to help overcome a problem or the need to adjust to external changes or reports. However, a central part of any evaluation has to be the means through which it can improve the management of the school.

This brings self-evaluation close to in-service training. The clue to effectiveness lies as much in the chance of implementing the ideas generated as in the ideas themselves. This accounts for the popularity of school-based in-service training. It increases the chances that the conclusions reached will be shared and relevant to the concrete situation. This is, of course, the problem with a book such as this. To implement any of the ideas means fitting them into the busy lives of teachers, into established routines. Books, documents, *aide-mémoire*, lists of questions, can present the idea; but it will remain academic until it is adjusted to the reality of schools. Similarly, teachers engaged in evaluating, record-keeping, or transition to secondary school produce new forms and new procedures, but may still see these unused, or ignored, unless the recommended process is built into the ongoing arrangements and teachers have an incentive to switch to them.

Stage 5: Improving Reliability and Validity. The initial steps in self-evaluation can be exciting. Under an enthusiastic headteacher or advisory service a school staff can produce reports and recommend changes on the basis of evidence accumulated. But the momentum can soon be lost. By the early 1980s many of the early voluntary schemes of self-evaluation sponsored by LEAs were only memories in the schools that were supposed to be involved, even though the scheme had since become the subject of academic articles, books and courses.

The lesson of these early attempts seems to me to be that modesty and parsimony are most likely to succeed. Picking the aspect of the school where the least investment of effort will yield the greatest improvement and then evaluating it is the simplest way to start off, and is unlikely to exhaust the teachers involved. Once the initial evaluation has been made, the cycle of stages outlined in this chapter can be gone through to improve it next time round, or when the next aspect is looked at. This means asking the questions about reliability and validity in Chapter 1, and repeating the steps recommended for pruning, amending and reinforcing. Thinking of self-evaluation as a continuing cycle can sustain the momentum. Once it is routine it is less threatening. But it still needs reviewing and improving as experience increases among the staff.

7 EVALUATING ASPECTS OF SCHOOL ORGANISATION

Whether the emphasis of in-school evaluation is on the professional development of teachers or the achievement of specified levels of pupil performance, on the curriculum or on internal communications or external relations, the priority is the same; improvement in the effectiveness of the school as an organisation. Schools have been organised to achieve more than keeping children off the streets. When specific aspects are evaluated the whole organisation has to be considered. The improvement of staff skills, of curriculum, of communications and so on are not ends in themselves, or separable from each other. They form part of the school as an organisation, and are evaluated to enable them to be managed to secure effectiveness in whatever the staff are, implicitly or explicitly, trying to achieve. Much evaluation does have the appearance of being an end in itself, or justified as self-evidently a good thing. This is reinforced by fashion. There is mileage in evaluation in the 1980s as there was in curriculum development in the 1960s. But evaluation is for use, for improving the organisation of learning.

Once this view, that evaluation is one useful way of improving the management of the school, is taken, it is possible to define the model that is held implicitly by teachers and bring it into the open to maximise its use. First, teachers are capable of specifying broad aims (Ashton, 1975). Secondly, they accept that the attainment of these aims is not wholly within their control. The social background of the pupils, and particularly the support of parents, are seen as important alongside the impact of schooling. Thirdly, teachers stress the need for adequate resources to support their curriculum and their own teaching style. But they also recognise as a fourth factor that their pupils bring into school very different abilities, and are motivated to use these in different ways. Hence the fifth aspect of this implicit model is that the outputs from schooling are the product of both school organisation and of pupil characteristics related to social background.

This model in the mind of teachers has backing from research. Attainment is affected by factors in the child's background, even if different schools achieve different levels of success with similar pupils. The model can be made explicit as follows:

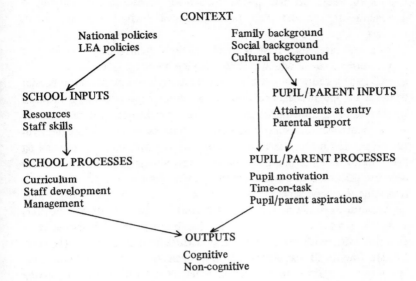

(This is a simplified model based on that presented by Glasman and Biniaminov (1981) derived from evidence on the relation between inputs and outputs in schools.)

From this model the important aspects of school organisation can be identified and related. That is the advantage of seeing the school as an organisation; it avoids evaluating bits and pieces as if they were separable. What children learn is affected not only by teaching but by their background, by the resources available, by the support they receive in the home. Evaluating the curriculum is a favourite exercise. Yet it is misleading to judge it in isolation from the learning experiences of children outside the school, from the extra-curriculum that extends learning on to playing field and into the community, and from the hidden curriculum where children learn from each other and from the unintended but powerful influences in the close-packed, tightly organised social arrangements in the school.

The selection of topics for evaluation that follow on pages 109 to 120 are arbitrary in two senses. First, they are selected from many important aspects of school organisation. Secondly, school organisation can be evaluated as a whole, not in parts. Probably the most cost-effective way of using the time of teachers is first to review the school as a means to achieve ends. This may lead to specifying aims and objectives. It may lead to evaluating particular aspects. The value in all cases is that staff are attempting to distance themselves from the hustle of teaching to consider what they are doing and why it is being done in that way.

In a few cases staff have worked out sophisticated lists of objectives and criteria against which success can be assessed (see, for example, Clark, 1981). More commonly, they have broken into working groups to look at specific aspects; but in all cases a point is soon reached where the evaluation needs to be structured to keep up the momentum and to move beyond snap judgements. Here the steps recommended in Chapter 2 are useful, particularly the introductory clarification. Being clear about what is being evaluated, the methods to be used and the way the information obtained is to be used, will ensure that everyone is reviewing the same aspect.

A useful example of the way evaluation can be built up in schools is available from the experience in Cambridgeshire primary schools experimenting with self-evaluation in a three-year programme (Prosser, 1982). One head explained the approach this way, 'Much of self-evaluation is plain common sense. What we are really doing is setting up a forum for sharing experience so that we can construct a guideline which people can understand and apply' (Hurlin in Prosser, 1982). Approaches in the schools included asking selected outsiders to give their views of the school, selection of a non-controversial area such as the use of space in the school to get evaluation started, and getting teachers to write down their expectations of pupils, comparing the results to uncover discrepancies. All the Cambridgeshire schools started with a common checklist of questions but soon developed their own procedures. Some LEA self-evaluation documents contain similar suggestions for getting started by rating priorities and the effectiveness of arrangements as seen by staff (for example, Solihull, 1980). In these schools as elsewhere, self-evaluation was open-ended. The checklist, or the survey of views about priorities or the selection of a concrete area for review acted as starter motor. Then the particular organisation of the school allowed staff to develop their own bespoke scheme. Some stayed at the whole school level, looking at aims and evaluating ethos. Others will rapidly get down to look at the action in the classrooms or elsewhere. Only one recommendation is possible. If you start with aims, do not forget the way they work out in practice in the school. If you start with the concrete, do not forget that it is supposed to lead somewhere.

The Use of Resources

It may seem suspiciously business-like to evaluate the way resources are used in a school. But even in the good times resources are scarce, and while decisions should be made on educational grounds, they need to take into account the benefits of allocating resources to one use rather than another. The decisions are about opportunity costs, for use here means that they are not available there. The tendency is to allocate resources as last year, with only minor adjustments; and this applies in central and local government as well as in schools. Yet this incrementalism can be unthinking, and can handicap the development of important areas of work while sustaining those that might have less value across the years, however important they were initially.

The review of resources is not only useful for balancing existing allocations but as a prelude to new developments. Particularly when resources are tight, new developments can only be financed from savings elsewhere. If staff are to attend courses their teaching has to be covered; if new materials are to be purchased someone else will not get theirs. Adopting self-evaluation means less time for curriculum development. Consideration of opportunity costs would have avoided many of the mistakes made in the heady days of curriculum projects in the 1960s. Not one evaluation of such projects included any consideration of costs. Yet teachers, like decision-makers in central and local government, consider these first. If innovation is at the expense of valued ongoing activities, the balance of advantages is likely to mean retrenchment.

The tendency to conservatism in organisations can be through inertia. But it can also come from a careful weighing of costs. Such a balance involves asking about aims, priorities, concrete objectives as well as the means for achieving them. It means looking for criteria against which different competing schemes can be assessed. Thus, once again, evaluating the use of resources leads to a consideration of the school as an organisation established to achieve ends that may often be implicit, but which are brought into the open through evaluation. To resolve even the most concrete of issues, the most profound of professional philosophies may be involved. Structuring the evaluation at least ensures that alternatives are considered and assumptions uncovered.

The simplest way of setting about this evaluation is to borrow LEA questions. Here are a few examples:

When was the allocation of space last reviewed? By whom was it reviewed, and is review necessary? (Solihull, 1980, p. 12).

Is there a written statement concerning approach to teaching and general organisation? (Salford, 1977, p. 8).
Who ensures that displays in the halls and corridors are well mounted and frequently changed? (Oxfordshire, 1979, p. 9).

These are satisfactory for a quick judgement, but do not open up the organisation of the school to scrutiny. Behind that organisation are assumptions about education. They may rarely be made explicit; they may never be reviewed. To do this requires a picture of the way resources are used in the school. This picture is often only available to the headteacher. Sharing the information about the allocation of capitation and of teaching loads is a way of facing teachers with the costs of possible ways of organising the school. Obviously there is no case for equality of teaching load or of resources, yet very often there is no consideration of the way work is allocated. This means that children within some classes may be receiving far less attention than those elsewhere. There should be an educational reason for the allocation of teacher and material resources, but this is likely to be assumed, not evaluated, if some simple indicator is not available.

This consideration of the attention given to children points to another often neglected aspect of school organisation. What resources are allocated to this group of children compared with that? Resources are given to schools on the assumption that they not only raise attainment generally, but do this without excessive inequality. Yet we know that the inequality persists and is detectable from an early age. Here the model in Figure 2.1 is again important. It may be little use allocating resources without regard for the context of schooling and the inputs brought in by children. Allocating resources available to the school involves consideration of causal links between outputs and processes, inputs and contexts.

The most common concerns are with the attainment of working-class compared with middle-class pupils, girls compared with boys, ethnic minorities compared with whites. A mundane decision to evaluate can bring the most profound problem facing schooling into focus once again. This is not neglected in LEA documents. Here is an example from the ILEA's *Keeping the School Under Review* (ILEA, 1977, p. 2).

In considering the needs and interests of individual children what provision is there for:
gifted children?

children who are slow to learn?
children with behaviour problems?
children for whom English is a second language?
children from different ethnic backgrounds?
children who have a specific skill or talent?

However, the impossibility of answering such questions without reference to some model of what causes low attainment can now be appreciated. Evaluation is context-bound and tied up with professional assumptions. When teachers believed in innate intelligence, fixed at an early age for life, they would make very different decisions about resource allocation from when they came to believe in the power of the environment to raise ability and performance. Some part of self-evaluation should be devoted to examining these more profound aspects that lie under questions about concrete issues. Unless they are evaluated the exercise is likely to remain cosmetic.

Staff Development

The evaluation of the professional development of staff may be a sensitive matter, but if it is claimed that a good school rests on good teachers then it must have priority. Human as well as material resources need to be used to best effect. The pay-off is not only in improving the effectiveness of the teaching. A review of the staff skills required to carry the chosen curriculum and of the necessary professional development necessitates a close look at the roles that teachers are playing in the school. Here evaluation is not only in context, but the context has itself to be evaluated. Further, professional development is an individual right for teachers. It becomes more important when the schools are contracting, and promotion and job opportunities are restricted.

There is then a sequence for evaluating staff development arising out of its place in the organisation of the school.

(1) The definition of the roles that teachers are expected to play in the organisation of the school and the relation between them.
(2) The review of staff requirements and performance.
(3) The organisation of school-based and external staff-development programmes to maintain and improve professional competence.

The Definition of Staff Roles

There is an extraordinary variety in the way procedures and responsibilities are defined and disseminated in schools. This school has a
'Blue Book' in which the responsiblities of teachers are clearly laid
down. It is given to teachers on appointment and is referred to when
the headteacher discusses organisation with the staff. In it are general
duties of the staff and the responsibilities of post-holders. Yet in a
neighbouring school there are no written job descriptions, and staff
pick up procedures by seeing what others do. Scaled posts have titles,
but are performed without definition. When the organisation is
changed, new jobs are allocated on a personal basis. Neither school is
necessarily well or badly organised. The definition of staff roles is the
organisation of the school, and a tight ship and a relaxed one may still
be effective.

LEA self-assessment documents contain a clear preference for the
tight ship:

Is the management structure appropriate and effective?

(Stockport, 1982 No. 4, p. 2.)

Is the school
(a) recognising its problems and weaknesses?
(b) working towards solutions to problems and weaknesses?

(Salford, 1977, p. 9)

The introduction of post-holders, particularly in middle schools,
has increased the need to review the responsibilities involved. In the
late 1960s the primary school teacher was seen as a generalist, and
integration of subjects was the vogue. Increasingly, however, HMIs
have been stressing the need for specialist staff, particularly in mathematics and science, to take specialist responsibility throughout primary
and middle schools for subject areas. The intention is that these teachers
should keep up to date in their subject, negotiate the curriculum,
produce materials, and give advice to colleagues. This is a new role in
primary schools. Definition is not easy, and tensions are likely. All such
specialist roles require definition and evaluation. Here, for example, are
a few questions from LEA self-assessment documents:

How does the staff of the school develop its professional competence?

(Stockport, 1982, Unit 4, p. 1.)

The human resources are so distributed that they serve the best interests of the school.
The fullest use is made of individual expertise among the staff.
Tasks are re-allocated from time to time.

(Solihull, 1980, p. 1.)

What are the specific responsibilities of senior members of staff other than the Head?   (Salford, 1977, p. 10.)

The position of the post-holder trying to get colleagues to change their practices in a subject area in which they may have been teaching for many years, is typical of the way tension can be generated in even a small, intimate school. The tendency in such schools is for the head-teacher to rely on informal talk in a common room to ensure that everyone knows what they are supposed to be doing and how relations are to be arranged. But informality is no guarantee of co-ordination or of adequate internal communication. A review of the procedures used can avoid misunderstandings. Such a review is dependent on asking 'who is responsible for what' questions. Here are examples from an LEA document:

What are the duties of those teachers who have posts of responsibility?
(a) Does the staff generally know of these duties?
(b) Are these duties revised from time to time?
(c) Do they meet the needs of the school – especially the curriculum?
(d) Is there a policy for identifying and developing the skills of post-holders?
(e) Who is responsible for the care of probationary teachers?

(Oxfordshire, 1979, p. 10.)

Reviewing Staff Requirements and Performance
There is always embarrassment over an in-school evaluation programme that includes teaching performance in the classroom. The steps outlined in Chapter 6 are essential, particularly full consultation to obtain the co-operation of staff in advance. The programme can also be started with volunteers. In many schools, particularly where there is team teaching or open planning, teachers are used to doing their job in the view of others. It is also the most important practical aspect of teacher training, for qualified teacher status is granted after a recommendation based on the observation by staff of students teaching. It occasionally happens in schools when inspectors or advisors call. Many headteachers

slip in to see how things are going, and this is necessary in the induction year to be able to affirm that probation should be ended.

There are a variety of ways in which teachers can receive some detached observation of their strengths and weaknesses where it matters. It can be arranged on a mutual basis between friends. The headteacher can establish it as routine. There are a number of self-rating scales. Examples from one of these follow (Sale, 1979, p. 166). It uses a 4-point scale from A for 'Excellent' to D for 'Poor, needs improvement' to check 33 questions.

1. Do I create a happy, relaxed, but business-like atmosphere?
2. Is order and control inherent in my approach to classroom management?
3. Am I conscious of each student's potentials and needs?

The key to removing the tension and maximising the usefulness is to look at the organisation of learning rather than the teaching performance. A very useful set of evidence can be found in the reports of the ORACLE project, where types of teaching are related to types of pupils' responses (Galton and Simon, 1980, pp. 181–212). The HMI primary survey also contains valuable comments on the way work is matched to children's abilities (DES, 1978). Other sources are research reports, such as Southgate on the way the extension of reading skill is organised (Southgate, Arnold and Johnson, 1981), and the many studies of classroom organisation (Stubbs and Delamont, 1976).

All these studies show how time and effort are divided up in samples of primary school classrooms. This evidence can serve as the basis of staff discussions for looking at the organisation of learning. It can also focus attention for self-evaluation or peer evaluation.

Teaching is, however, more than organising learning in the classroom. Teachers have worries, ambitions, hopes. These need to be discussed so that they may develop professionally. This evaluation has to be a two-way procedure. A teacher may be having discipline problems with a class. Discussing it with the headteacher will be seen as a sign of weakness unless the discussion is seen as routine, engaged in by all. The problem is also the headteacher's and other teachers' concern. They are there to support, and the teacher has a claim on them. In the school-based schemes the teacher volunteers to participate in self-evaluation. He or she discusses present and future with the headteacher or a senior member of the staff. This is structured to enable the teacher to ask questions as well as answer them. The agenda is best worked out in advance with the staff, and the outcome of the evaluation sessions should be a plan for future professional development, whether internal or external. The teacher has the right to expect a response as well as having a duty to respond. Such routine professional evaluations ensure that references, promotions and future evaluations are based on firm evidence. If staff agree that a summary should be produced and agreed between the parties, it will serve as a basis for these assessments.

It is here that the question 'who evaluates the evaluator?' becomes important. It is no use uncovering the problems of a teacher if support from colleagues is not forthcoming. It is no use having the headteacher involved in talking to staff about remedies if it is his or her own short-comings that account for the complaint. The risk to a teacher displaying genuine honesty in an interview about lack of support or effective management is obvious. Furthermore, improvements in adverse situations are unlikely unless staff development is part of a broader review of school organisation.

The Maintenance and Improvement of Skills

The report by HMI *Education 5 to 9* (DES, 1982) was one of a line of reports stressing the need for in-service training. In the report on the education of the 5 to 9s special emphasis was placed on the need to train headteachers, and teachers with special responsibilities. Only 18 heads out of the 80 schools reviewed were found to encourage teachers to develop special interests and expertise. In only eight cases were they encouraged to visit other schools. The tendency for teachers to draw on the same skills while the organisation of schooling changes is sufficient reason for including in-service training in evaluation.

In-service training need not consist of going on courses. It is necessary to review the available opportunities organised by LEA, DES or academic institutions. Headteachers may want to be responsible for collecting the information together, or to ask a colleague to take respon-sibility. But school-based in-service training is often more rewarding. The act of reviewing a curriculum area, or teaching arrangements, or classroom management, through staff working parties can lead to improving the skills that can be brought to bear, particularly if advisors can be persuaded to help in the organisation, or a member of staff can provide the agenda and the documentation. The key to any approach is the commitment to review and develop, and it is often more effective to do this in the particular context of the school.

The evaluation of arrangements for updating staff skills should also cover the collection, distribution and discussion of current developments. The flood of reports from the DES, from HMIs, from the APU has added to the steady accumulation of research findings. Yet teachers may read little of this evidence. Have you read one of the regular reports from the APU? Have you read any of the HMI 'Matters of Concern' series, or the primary survey, or the 5 to 9 report? Teachers are busy people and need help to keep up with the literature. Reviewing the means through which this might be made easier can lead to someone taking responsibility for collecting together accounts of current reports, or to this responsibility being shared out among teachers with different interests so they can share their information.

Finally, the evaluation of staff performance should include discussion of career development. This involves more than the improvement of skills to do the current job. It covers the possibilities for promotion within the school and to other schools. Particularly where staff evaluation is based on regular interviews with the headteacher or other senior staff, prospects should be discussed along with the preparation and experience required. The mutual benefit from such evaluation of both potential and prospects is obvious. The individual teacher benefits from the advice, and the school benefits from the raising of the levels of competence.

Community and School Relations

The model at the start of this chapter directs attention to the importance of factors outside the school in determining the performance of pupils within it. The implementation of the 1980 Education Act in 1982 has forced schools and LEAs to release basic information. But many schools are actively engaging parents in the classroom and trying to open up the school to the community. Reviewing community-school relations once again involves very profound issues concerning the way teachers see their professional role. Hence it would be misleading to concentrate on concrete issues and ignore the fundamental question 'why do we need to establish good relations with parents and the community?'

The first important point for starting on self-evaluation of public relations is the evidence that there has been no collapse of parental confidence in schooling. This has been found in London in 1976–7 (Johnson and Ransom, 1980) and in Birmingham in 1976 (Tomlinson, 1980). Furthermore, the parents interviewed were very concerned about their children's education. This survey evidence is supported in the East Sussex Accountability in the Middle Years of Schooling study (Becher, Eraut and Knight, 1981). Here parents did worry. They wanted information about the things that concerned their children, but overall they saw contemporary primary schooling as a pleasant experience for most children and a marked change for the better when compared with their own school days. Thus, evaluation does not need to start from a position of crisis.

A first step is to review the existing written communications. Most LEA documents on self-evaluation for schools contain convenient questions or statements.

Does the school have a prospectus or handbook for new parents?
Are the contents of the school's handbook to parents as informative and up to date as they can be?
Is there a periodic newsletter to parents?   (Lancashire)

Communications are couched in language which is easily understood by parents.   (Solihull)

However, such questions tend to be free from the context of total communication. An alternative start might be to review existing practices and decide which model seems to have been adopted, whether intentionally or not. In research conducted by the School of Education at the University of Nottingham, four models are proposed for written communications, each with distinctive features (Bastiani, 1978). These four are as follows:

1. The Basic Information Model – here a limited range of factual information is transmitted to parents. The role of the parents is to receive it as ignorant amateurs.
2. The Public Relations Model – here the objective is to persuade, obtain agreement, avoid conflict. The school tries to project an image, tailor it to the needs of the intended audience and ensure through the presentation that the message will get across.
2a. The 'E.P.A. Primary' Model – here the emphasis is on trying to convince parents of the value of social relevance and pastoral care, while trying to convince the LEA and other funding agencies of the need for extra resources.
2b. The 'Academic Recruitment' Model – here the effort is put into recruiting motivated children through a stress on staff qualifications, academic curriculum, school uniform and good behaviour.

3. The Developmental Model — here the information provided is to help over entry and transfer, with an emphasis on supporting parents at what may be a difficult time.

4. The Parental Involvement Model — here the attempt is to provide information that will create a broader, deeper relationship with parents through a stress on openness and partnership.

The connection to the views of staff about their professional role is clear. If the staff collectively conclude that education is more effective if there is parental support and involvement, then the fourth model should be the guide to external communications. In this model, in addition to the standard needs for clarity, good appearance and a welcoming tone, there should be educational as distinct from purely administrative content. Cynics may suggest that such communications will not be read, that meetings called to discuss educational matters are poorly attended, and that parents do not give adequate support to the teachers of their own children. The East Sussex Accountability project found evidence of these attitudes. Teachers did seem to feel that parents were not looking after their children properly. Certainly, the parental concerns were narrow, mainly about the way mathematics and English were being taught. But parents still wanted that information, while teachers were convinced that the efforts they were making to explain things to parents were not appreciated. The available evidence suggests that parents prefer interviews with individual teachers, but they also want detailed prospectuses and a school report. They do not rate highly general talks about the curriculum.

When teachers evaluate their external relations the whole range of activities relating to the community have to be considered. It may be useful to start with the documents sent out because these can be most readily improved. The arrangements for meetings with parents are clearly central to the interests of all parties, and such a review has a high priority. It helps to keep a record of attendance at various kinds of meetings to accumulate a picture of the popular activities to help in the review. But from there the evaluation should proceed to broader issues about the means and kinds of the education being offered.

There is evidence that the proportion of schools with some form of parent-teacher association has increased over the last decade. In the Plowden survey 17 per cent of primary schools had such an association (Plowden, 1967). In a survey by the NFER in 1976-7 the proportion had increased to 35 per cent, with another 26 per cent having a less formal committee (Clift, 1979). But this leaves 40 per cent with no association. This does not necessarily mean that parents are not welcome; three-quarters of the schools in the NFER survey involved parents in some school activities. But there are clearly questions to ask about the perceived role of parents in the school.

Finally, it is necessary to widen the scope of the questions to look at the relation between the school and the communities around it. Staff need not be committed to the idea of community education in any of its versions to give high priority to ensuring that no group of children is being handicapped by lack of information or welcome. This is particularly important where the school serves an area containing ethnic minorities. On the evidence from Birmingham there is no widespread dissatisfaction among minorities (Tomlinson, 1980), but West Indian and Asian parents were concerned about teachers who did not seem to them to get down to the business of teaching literacy and numeracy, and who seemed lax in maintaining discipline. In many LEAs there have been efforts to provide information and contacts to overcome any lack of communication that could account for this feeling. But it is teachers who eventually have to tackle the problem.

However, it would be wrong to concentrate on ethnic minorities. There is sufficient evidence of low attainment among the children of semi-skilled and unskilled working-class parents to include their involvement with the school in any review of external relations. Part of the reason for the low attainment may be that the parents are not in a position to help their children as easily as richer parents from better-housed areas. It is very easy to make inarticulate parents ill at ease at meetings, or to word reports and brochures in a way that patronises or baffles them.

Perhaps the most promising way forward for teachers reviewing external relations is to call on outsiders to help. The customers should be able to help in saying what is needed. There may be interested parties among the governors. The local minority communities are often organised to provide a representative. The LEA might have specialist advisors. Neighbouring schools might be willing to share external monitoring, so that teachers from the two staffrooms can act as consultant and auditor for each other. In no other area of the work of the school does it seem so promising to involve outsiders to advise.

This chapter on the evaluation of the school as an organisation began with a model that reflected the way teachers see the various factors involved. Even when specific aspects such as the use of material or human resources are being reviewed, they are looked at, implicitly or explicitly, with such a model in mind. My own view is that it is more useful to make things explicit, and review not only communications with parents, or assessment procedures, or transfer arrangements or whatever is chosen for evaluation, but the way such aspects affect other parts of the school as an organisation. Some thought should also be given to the way review and action for improvement might affect the more intangible but important perspective of the school as a whole, its climate, feeling, ethos.

The depth at which the review is operated can range from an unstructured discussion between staff, or a fully structured evaluation as detailed in Chapter 6. But in all cases the school should be conceived as an organisation, receiving material and teaching resources and allocating them to help children learn. That is why the model at the start of this chapter is useful, for it includes the factors within and outside the school that affect that learning. Self-evaluation can become piecemeal, focused on a particular problem or aspect without reference to the school as a whole, or to what staff are trying to achieve. Once again, evaluation is a means to ends worked out by staff, not an end in itself.

8 EVALUATING THE CURRICULUM

There have been three approaches to curriculum evaluation. The first has concentrated on the effectiveness of different arrangements, the success in attaining specified objectives, or the illumination of the way the learning has been organised (see, for example, Hamilton, 1976). The second, best illustrated in the seven 'Blocks' of the Open University's *Curriculum in Action* course P234 (Open University, 1982b), concentrates on the effectiveness of classroom activities. The first misses the detail that can lead to on-the-spot improvements, and tends to ignore what children are actually doing. The second misses the opportunity to check that the curriculum is really worthwhile, and tends to ignore what it might be best for the children to be doing. School-based curriculum evaluation may be focused mainly on improving the way things are taught. But it also needs to scan the balance, the relevance, the continuity and the fairness of what is taught. Thus, the third approach is not to concentrate on the effectiveness of curricula or the way they are taught, but on their relevance, utility and justice. Once again, the review can range from a staff discussion about the curriculum as a whole or about specific aspects, to the careful specification of aims as a start of a controlled criterion, norm or self-referenced evaluation. In practice teachers continually review and change the curriculum. As part of the development of the course, the Schools Council *Curriculum in Action* team worked with teachers, and finished with six questions. These were as follows:

What did the pupils actually do?
What were they learning?
How worthwhile was it?
What did I do?
What did I learn?
What do I intend to do now?

Reviewing the curriculum can mean anything from describing what is supposed to be learned, or how it is taught, the balance, continuity, relevance or worth of the content, or the benefits that accrue to pupils. Some clarification is required, and the first step is once again to decide what is to be evaluated, how this is to be done, and how the results are to be used for improvements.

Four aspects of the curriculum can be identified to help structure evaluation. There is *content*, recently the subject of publications by the DES (1980a and 1981), HMI (DES, 1980b). and Schools Council (1981a). Secondly, there is the *organisation* of the curriculum, focused on the relation between subjects, continuity within them and the way they are taught. Thirdly, evaluation can concentrate on the *situation* for which the curriculum has been organised, and the way it serves children and community. Lastly, there can be some attempt to evaluate *impact*, linking evaluation of the school as an organisation to the evaluation of the work of pupils.

The Content of the Curriculum

In a survey of teachers' responses to the 'Great Debate' in the late 1970s, Wicksteed and Hill (1979) found teachers to be unworried about the discussions of primary school curricula. They were in favour of core curricula in mathematics and English which would lay down the common elements, but still leave scope for individual approaches. In these 'vehicle' subjects teachers seem to acknowledge that variations should be limited. HMIs found that over four-fifths of primary schools had written schemes of work in these basic areas (DES, 1978). Teachers seem to have acted in advance of advice from the centre. In the 'tapestry' subjects, where HMIs found just over a third of the primary schools surveyed with written schemes of work, teachers in the Wicksteed and Hill survey still welcomed broad indications of the work they should include. The assessment by teachers of their own curriculum content, even against externally produced guidelines such as the two DES statements (DES, 1980a and 1981) and the HMI statement (DES, 1980b) is not likely to produce anything very dramatic. Nevertheless, self-evaluation can be useful. The curriculum can become crowded and superficial. It can omit important areas such as science and study skills. It can incorporate values which are insulting to some children and meaningless to others. It can be unfair because it contains assumptions that have not been made explicit and thought through. The action taken after evaluation may only involve changes around the margin, but they may make a lot of difference to some children and their parents. Furthermore, the DES in *The School Curriculum* (DES, 1981) asked for a regular review of curricula in schools, and said that they would be asking LEAs about responses to the proposals they had made.

The need to see curriculum evaluation as a first step to action links this chapter to the rest. Very often the identification of an area that is strong or weak, that needs contraction or expansion, necessitates staff development, a re-allocation of available resources, negotiations with LEA, or putting parents in the picture. There is nothing new in this evaluation. Teachers are continually adjusting the content of their work to take account of the impression that they have of events inside and outside the school. LEAs, through the advisory service, are trying to influence schools. They may also be initiating self-evaluation through an *aide-mémoire* or evaluation booklets. Teachers are scanning and spotting problems, and taking action to overcome them. Research, whether from academia, the LEA, or the DES is producing evidence on gaps, developments, strengths and weaknesses in the curriculum. Academics are also busy analysing the curriculum and producing models for development. There is no shortage of material against which to reference curriculum evaluation within a school.

A most useful document is the Schools Council's *The Practical Curriculum* (Schools Council, 1981a). This is written as a set of problems rather than as a prescription, and each chapter ends with a checklist to help teachers question their own arrangements. The approach used is to first discuss very general aims and to proceed to break these down. Practically, they start with the aims stated in the *Warnock Report* (Warnock, 1978). These were firstly,

to enlarge a child's knowledge, experience and imaginative understanding, and thus his awareness of moral values and capacity for enjoyment: and secondly, to enable him to enter the world after formal education is over as an active participant in society and a responsible contributor to it, capable of achieving as much independence as possible.

In a similar fashion, HM Inspectorate have produced *A View of the Curriculum* (DES, 1980b), the DES *A Framework for the School Curriculum* (DES, 1980a) and *The School Curriculum* a year later (DES, 1981). HMIs have the advantage of the data from their national surveys, and see the curriculum as the product of the assumptions of teachers. Like the Schools Council, they present ways through which teachers can check these assumptions in their own schools.

Much of the official thinking about the content of the curriculum has been influenced by academics. Hirst's philosophical approach has been particularly influential. He identified seven forms of knowledge, empirical, mathematical, philosophical, moral, aesthetic, religious, historical/sociological (Hirst, 1974). Hirst expressed some doubts about the last category, but the remainder are seen as logically independent with distinctive tests for validating the propositions in each. In another attempt to outline areas of knowledge that all children should experience, Whitfield (1978) settles for the following subject areas for school: languages, mathematics, natural sciences, creative subjects, human studies (domestic science, economics, civics, physical education etc.) and humanities (geography, history, religious studies, moral education).

It will now be clear that content is unlikely to differ dramatically between schools although the emphasis and time allocated will. For example, HMIs found 36 curriculum aspects which were found, individually, in over 80 per cent of primary school classes inspected in the mid-1970s (DES, 1978). The influence of academic thinking on official prescriptions has been important. For example, the APU in its early days worked with a model of six curriculum areas: language, mathematics, science, personal and social development, aesthetic development and physical development. These lines of development were chosen because they seemed to offer a balanced picture of the whole curriculum and the possibility of checking performance across all curriculum objectives.

Here is a typical sequence for a holistic evaluation of the curriculum. It is taken from the Cheshire Curriculum Reappraisal Group's report (Cheshire Education Committee, 1981) on their part of the collaboration between LEAs, HMIs and teachers in five local authorities to find out means whereby teachers could reappraise their curriculum, using the breakdown into areas of experience presented in the HMI 'Red Book', *Curriculum 11-16* (DES, 1977). The analyses was prepared by teachers under the following headings:

1. Aims
2. Objectives – concepts: ideas that help pupils organise, understand etc.
   – skills: techniques to practise or master
   – attitudes: derived from inner feelings and developed through the various school disciplines
   – content/knowledge
3. Method – teaching strategies for achieving objectives
4. Assessment – of pupils' performance in relation to objectives
5. Evaluation – of courses and organisation of learning.

It was recommended that this analysis of the work of the staff should be undertaken each year. Teachers were to agree on action after the analysis. There is controversy over these holistic approaches through aims and objectives, since they are time-consuming, and can produce information that is somewhat divorced from reality. It is also very difficult to break down aims into assessable objectives and to agree on criteria for judging success in achieving them. But the effort can be rewarding, for planning to evaluate the work of the school as a whole incorporates thinking about where it is supposed to be guiding pupils. The act of evaluating may be just as rewarding as any final evaluation. If there is clarification, a sorting out of priorities and agreement between staff so that a common policy is thrashed out, the absence of precise criteria for evaluating particular objectives can be of secondary importance. There is a danger in aims remaining implicit for this can lead to the criticism that the school is aimless.

Most LEA suggestions for curriculum evaluation are pragmatic. Here are examples from LEA self-evaluation documents:

What are the School's aims and objectives for its pupils?
How is the Curriculum intended to fulfil them?
How far does it fulfil them?
Does it provide a coherent programme for each pupil?
(Stockport, 1982, Unit 2, p. 1.)

Rate the importance and effectiveness of the school's schemes of work.   (Solihull, 1980, p. 32)

These questions are usually produced by teachers and advisors sitting as a working party, and consequently are an explication of the sort of questions that teachers implicitly ask of themselves. This makes such lists of questions easy to use. It is likely, however, that they incorporate assumptions about what the curriculum should include, not just neutral questions. Different questions could lead to different answers. If each school caters for a different locality, it may require a different curriculum from its neighbours, even though the differences are likely to be small.

Organising the Curriculum

It is doubtful if the fuss over the guidance given by the DES over the content of the school curriculum was worthwhile, given the very few schools which would not have included every item in the lists provided (DES, 1980a). The alternative lists provided by HMIs (DES, 1980b), the Schools Council (Schools Council, 1981a) and by many academics were also remarkable for their similarity. Indeed, with staff being cut as school rolls fell, decisions over what to include and exclude were increasingly determined by the teachers available rather than by any choice of an ideal curriculum. Staffing by curriculum also meant curriculum by staffing.

Unfortunately, this debate, concentrated on the rights of central government to have a say in curriculum matters rather than on the content itself, took attention away from the often more important questions about the way the learning in schools was organised. As all but a few schools included the curriculum recommended, the more important question was usually about the organisation needed to enable children to master the key areas and have continuity in their learning. Here are four aspects of curriculum organisation that are rarely evaluated, yet can bring large returns for small investments of effort:

(1) The continuity in learning the basic skills across the years of learning

(2) The synchronisation of learning between the sequences in the different curriculum areas as discussed below

(3) The organisation of study skills to ensure that learning in key areas is not held up

(4) Adequate preparation through the curriculum for transition between schools, whether to secondary school or resulting from parents moving house.

Here is the model produced with a group of primary school teachers looking at aspects (1) to (4). Obviously there was no way of detailing all the steps even in the basic skills selected for evaluation, so the group worked out the position in the career of children when key aspects would be covered. These were selected because they were important within reading and mathematics, but also because they were necessary skills for learning elsewhere in the curriculum. Their timing as well as sequence had to be considered. The selection of study skills was another example of making the implicit explicit. Skills, such as looking up references, using a dictionary, speedy extraction of information from a book, using a pocket calculator, were acknowledged as important, but were not timetabled. The decision to make sure that they were, preceded the evaluation of curriculum continuity and linking.

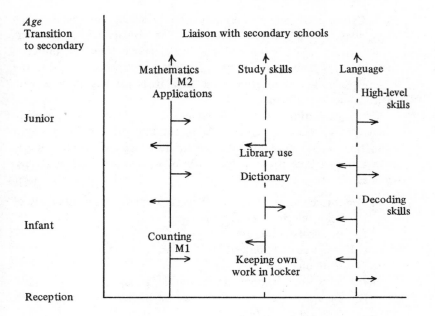

Examples M1: Can count any set up to 9 objects. Can read, write and order numerals 0–9.
M2: Knows meaning of % notation as used in simple, everyday situations.

The evaluation of arrangements for transition to secondary schools has lain behind many recent efforts to improve the complicated situation in many large secondary school systems. In Inner London in the 1970s there were schools receiving children from over 60 primary schools. Curiously, there were costly innovations, such as teachers who brought top juniors with them to the secondary school every other year, taught them there and returned to teach another form of top juniors the following year. In cost-effective terms the linking of the primary to the secondary school curriculum might have been more rewarding. Secondary school teachers of mathematics in particular complained that they had to spend a year bringing the children from all the different primary schools up to the same starting line before moving on to the secondary curriculum. Most secondary schools set a reading test on entry at 11 years, despite receiving such a score on most records from the primary schools. The ILEA designed the special *London Reading Test* (ILEA, 1979) to try to avoid this duplication. Usually the initiative for some synchronisation came from secondary school staff, but this could look like an attempt to dictate to primary school teachers, particularly when negotiated from a specialist viewpoint. The primary schools teachers in the group which produced the model above took the initiative themselves by listing what they saw as the key aspects covered in the primary school, and offering these as a basis for negotiations with their secondary colleagues.

The organisation of the curriculum is of course of immediate concern to LEAs and it would be expected that their booklets on self-evaluation would contain questions on the aspects covered above. Here are questions from *Keeping the School under Review* (ILEA, 1977, p. 4):

1. Has the school programmes of work or guidelines in all or any of the following areas of the curriculum:
   (a) physical education?
   (b) language and literacy?
   (c) mathematics?
   (d) aesthetic developments, e.g. music, art and crafts?
   (e) environmental studies, e.g. geography, history, social studies, physical and natural sciences?
   (f) religious and moral education?
2. When were the programmes drawn up?
   By whom were they made?
   When were they last revised?
   What advice was sought from any learning-support agencies?
   Which programmes now need revision?

Analysing the Curriculum Situation

The light in the eye of the children that serves as the indicator for much evaluation in the classroom is part of the continual exchange that takes place between teacher and learner. That exchange is organised by teachers with one eye on the work to be covered, the other on the responses of the children. The evaluation feeds information into curriculum re-planning. As the curriculum is analysed and attempts are made to improve it, the background of the children, of the school and of the community around it are taken into account. Skilbeck (1976) developed this situational analysis as central to curriculum as a reflection of culture, as relevant to the life of the children, for they bring into the classroom attitudes, values and skills that will shape their response to the teacher.

Here evaluation is necessary to ensure that the curriculum is not violating the beliefs of the children and that it is being reinforced by their experience outside school. This is not necessarily a plea for relevance. But even the most academic curriculum designed to provide a ticket out of the locality for the children will succeed only if the influences of the local community are taken into account. The necessary analysis is usually implicit. Once again, the objective here is to make that explicit and hence more effective.

Skilbeck separates the factors that have to be taken into account in a situational analysis into external and internal (Reynolds and Skilbeck, 1976, pp. 113-15). Among the external factors are changes in the economy and political life, expectations of parents and employers, community assumptions, the changing nature of school subjects, the support structure of schools such as teachers' centres, and the resources made available. Among the internal factors are pupil attitudes, abilities and values, the strengths and weaknesses of teachers, the school ethos and organisation, the material resources and the existing curriculum. This is a similar collection of factors to that in the model in Chapter 7 showing causal relationships within and outside the school.

There is a wealth of research on the environment from which children come and its influence on their learning. In the 1960s most of these studies were of different social class backgrounds (see, for examples, Douglas, 1964). In the 1970s the research switched to ethnic minorities, and attention was also focused on the way the curriculum could penalise girls. The need to appreciate the differences in the backgrounds of children is obvious, and it is now appreciated that the curriculum can penalise identifiable groups and account for their low attainment. There is no blueprint that can be followed in this curriculum evaluation. For every expert pressing a curriculum relevant to a poor community or to blacks, there is another supporting an academic curriculum that will enable all children to compete. Self-evaluation through a situational analysis is a way of ensuring that the curriculum does not leave too many children either bewildered or insulted.

Curriculum for a Multi-ethnic Society

This is a useful way of summarising the benefits and difficulties of assessing curriculum in schools. It is tempting to look at the curriculum for the multi-ethnic school. However, this is a limited view, for if the aim is to promote a harmonious community, appreciation of other people's way of life cannot be confined to those schools which have a mixed intake. The difficulties often lie with those who have little contact with people from other cultures. Across the 1970s the pressure grew to take into account that 'Our society is a multicultural, multiracial one and the curriculum should reflect a sympathetic understanding of the different cultures and races that make up our society' (DES, 1977). Simultaneously, there has been a shift from seeing the issue as special, to meet needs such as language requirements, to reappraising the curriculum to make it relevant to all pupils (Little and Willey, 1981).

However, while it may be widely agreed that the curriculum should be relevant to all children in a multicultural society, it is by no means agreed what this entails. The questions in LEA self-evaluation booklets go no further than asking general questions such as 'How are non-English speaking parents helped to participate in the life of the school and community? (Oxfordshire, 1979, p. 12).

There are, however, some guidelines. First, some children may need English as a second language, both in the initial phase and in continuing support for skills to be sustained and developed. Secondly, there is an EEC Directive that mother-tongue teaching should be made available. Part of the evaluation of the curriculum has to be concentrated on ensuring that no children are being penalised because they lack the necessary command of English, and the question about the availability of mother-tongue teaching should also be asked. But the answer may not allow action to be taken. Furthermore, many LEAs see no need for such teaching, although there is less of this negative attitude with reference to infant and junior school (Little and Willey, 1981, p. 20). There is a similar lack of unanimity over other aspects of the multicultural curriculum such as analysing and meeting the language needs of children of West Indian origin. Second, third and fourth generations of these children may be penalised in school because of their language, but there is no agreement on whether it is a problem, or what should be done about it. Indeed, the black community itself might reasonably object if the language of their children was deemed inadequate. The questions should be asked as the curriculum is evaluated. But teachers will find few agreed answers available beyond their own professional opinions.

The current view on the curriculum is that it should be permeated with an awareness of the multicultural society rather than have 'black studies' or 'religions of the world' or steel band practice tacked on.

Two-thirds of all schools in the Little and Willey survey had discussed this issue at staff meetings (Little and Willey, 1981, pp. 20-1). Where it had been discussed, it had led to only very general action. It might be necessary to go beyond agreeing that the 'ethos of the school' and 'across the curriculum approaches' should be affected, to asking another series of questions on what such statements really mean in practice. In *Education for a Multiracial Society*, The Schools Council (Schools Council, 1981b, p. 20) lists five criteria for selecting the learning experiences for the curriculum in a multiracial society. The curriculum needs to:

be global in content and perspective
have visuals, stories and information that show a variety of social and ethnic groups
give accurate information about racial and cultural differences and similarities
avoid stereotypes
avoid judgements against exclusively British or European norms.

These are the sorts of criteria against which an existing curriculum could be judged. The Schools Council can be criticised for emphasising racial rather than ethnic aspects in case this consolidates the concept of race and racial differences, but the list gives standards against which the content of teaching and of books can be evaluated. Hicks (1981, pp. 87-92) has gathered together a number of sources for evaluating learning resources. Each of these presents ways of scanning materials for discrimination. The questions reflect the concern built into the five criteria above. Thus a scan would include the following:

1. *Check the content* Are minorities a 'problem'? Are problems defined from a white, Anglo-Saxon, Christian, male, middle-class point of view? Are minorities shown as subservient, menial?
2. *Check the pictures* Are the heroes Bulldog Drummonds and the villains dagoes and blacks? Are blacks shown in authority? Is there just a token black face presented?
3. *Check the facts* Is the historical view of Britain as top nation or always in the right? Is the developing world displayed as a land of happy savages or simple farmers? Are the social and economic realities presented as explanations?

Obviously asking such questions may expose the grosser bias, but the line will be drawn in different places in different schools. First, there is a danger that efforts to improve the self-image of children from ethnic minorities might be patronising, or, even worse, handicap the very children that need support by reducing their time on academic tasks. Blacks need higher academic qualifications to get equivalent jobs when compared with whites, and this need should not be jeopardised. There is also the need to consider the majority and the positive benefits of a few lusty choruses of 'Land of Hope and Glory'. The Charge of the Light Brigade still stirs the blood, despite its pointlessness. Ethnocentrism is to be avoided; but a balance has to be attained so that the curriculum is not sterilised into boredom.

Fortunately there are excellent references to teaching materials (Schools Council, 1981b, pp. 165-97, and Hicks, 1981, pp. 113-22) and sources provided by those involved with minorities (Commission for Racial Equality, 1976; School of Oriental and African Studies, 1978) and organisations producing teaching materials such as the Afro-Caribbean Educational Resource Project, Bogle L'Ouverture Publications, the Oxfam Educational Department and the Islamic Foundation. One of the best ways of evaluating the curriculum and teaching materials is to ask representatives of the minority groups in the community around the school to give advice. This should extend over the whole curriculum, not just the sections specifically related to the minority cultures.

Finally, there are many minorities, and some of them attain at a low level. In reviewing curriculum the focus can be on minorities, on girls, or on the children of semi- or unskilled working-class parents, or on the very mobile, or those with learning difficulties, or the gifted. It can also be on minorities and others who tend to attain above average. The purpose of evaluating curriculum is to minimise injustice for all children, the very able as well as the less able, the poor as well as the rich.

Checking the Impact

Evaluating the effectiveness of different curricula has defeated most researchers. Dispute over reliability and validity has been the main outcome, and this has kept academics busy rather than informing teachers of best ways forward. Hence it is realistic to recommend that staff evaluate impact through their shared judgements, structured as far as possible by taking the steps described in Chapter 2. In the end the success of a curriculum has to be assessed against the performance of the children involved. In a few areas, such as the reading and mathematics curriculum, it is possible to get some data through standardised tests giving either a reference to national or other norms, or to criteria established by the test designers. Similarly, a school staff might store up test scores and check them over time.

In many areas of the curriculum such a quantitative approach is not feasible. Here professional judgement is necessary; and it can be supplemented by asking advisors, neighbouring teachers, parents and academics to add their judgements. Some schools have organised evaluation panels of outsiders to look at selected areas of work. Others have liaised with nearby schools to exchange evaluations. It is a brave step to ask outsiders 'how are we doing?', but the confidence can be established slowly with an educative effect on those involved within and without.

9 EVALUATING EDUCATIONAL PROGRAMMES

Most of this book is about evaluation as an integral part of the organisation of learning within the school. The techniques recommended have been derived from models of evaluation that are implicit in the way teachers go about their work. But there are occasions when teachers are more detached and ask 'is this way of organising, or teaching or innovating etc. effective?' They are posing the questions faced by evaluators of curriculum projects, or by researchers asked to investigate methods of treating delinquents, or natural scientists experimenting to investigate whether all living things breathe.

In education evaluation is usually concerned with new developments, and these can range from the radical to the marginal. Teachers evaluate these impressionistically. The criteria used for judging success may be ill defined, but are close to those used by researchers. It should be possible to use experience gained in evaluation to help teachers. Thus, this chapter contains suggestions for getting near the answer to the question 'is this really any good?', by setting about evaluation experimentally. This does not replace professional judgement, which is involved all the way. Neither does it replace the need to observe, illuminate, question, discuss and probe. Hence, there are suggestions for combining technical approaches with professional judgement so that the aspect under investigation is dealt with in depth and with breadth.

The start is with the basic, natural scientific control-group experiment shown in Figure 9.1. Most of us have investigated some of the characteristics of living things by this method. Here is the simplest example. First, we clean two gas jars, place marbles in one and the same weight of beans in the other. The jars are sealed, scrutinised for any initial differences, and then observed after the passage of time. Secure in the knowledge that the only difference in the two jars was the life in the beans, the conclusion can be drawn from the observation, after a passing of time, of mist on the glass around the beans, that these have given off water vapour. All other explanations seem to have been eliminated by the control exerted through the presence of the jar with only the marbles in it.

Fortunately, there are objections to treating individuals and particularly children experimentally. Thus, the fundamental control that is possible in the natural sciences is usually unethical in human science. This applies in school and classrooms. To obtain a controlled experiment to evaluate a teaching method, or curriculum, or form of organisation would require taking a large group of children and then allocating them at random to the experimental group which will experience the aspect under consideration, while the others act as controls. Sometimes it is possible to use a natural situation where there are already two groups, only one of which has been involved in an innovation. But the control has been lost over the experiment because we cannot be sure that other factors have not caused any differences that occur. There can be matching to check the similarity of the groups, but other factors may be present which could affect the results.

The design in Figure 9.2, looked at alongside the true control-group design, shows that there may be many more than one factor, the aspect under investigation, that could account for any differences between the testing or observation before and after the experiment took place. This applies in particular to the motivation or development of the children which can account for observed differences before and after. This is one factor that can be checked through the existence of a control group. It is difficult to draw conclusions relating the programme, experiment or development to changes detected by the observations before and after the event, without the control.

Figure 9.1: True Experimental Design Using Randomly Formed Groups

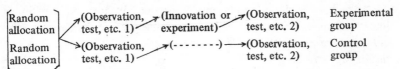

Figure 9.2: Before-and-after Design

This disadvantage in the before-and-after design is not all loss. It does fit naturally into the way teachers review their work. Its simplicity frees time for looking closely at what is going on, in addition to specific changes. The most useful package would be a development of this design that nevertheless had some control built in, without involving excessive extra work, or any disruptive re-organisation of ongoing procedures. All teachers use this design to judge how well their teaching or the new reading books or the new timetable are going. They often evaluate after the event, remembering rather than observing what went before, and then comparing that with what they see happening with the new arrangements. Very few teachers would think of designing a randomised control-group study to test whether the introduction of a pupil-completed checklist of books read improves reading performance, or whether behaviour will deteriorate if 'merit awards' are abandoned. Most compare their situation before and after a change. The most helpful way to build in some control and greater insight with the least work is to develop this everyday model in a similar way to the development of the formative evaluation model for pupils in Chapter 2.

Bearing the model in Figure 9.2 in mind, imagine a teacher wanting to know whether a new method of getting children to appreciate historical time is better than her usual way. The old method was to give the children six topics during the year, each from a different historical period and to relate them to each other, as they were completed, through discussion as the materials produced were displayed in the classroom. This method was replaced by the introduction of a frieze on the classroom wall with time stretched out from the birth of Christ to the present day. The number of topics and the discussion at the end of each remained the same. But as each was prepared and displayed it was 'placed' on the time-chart and its relation to other events, such as those introduced in religious education and music, was discussed and used as a basis for simple exercises for the children to complete using the library.

A teacher would normally introduce the new method, and judge improvement or deterioration through memory of performance on the old and impressions of the new. She uses a before-and-after design, but intuitively and usually without planning. For most changes in the organisation of learning that is all that is possible, for the job has to go on. But some aspects of learning are too important to leave to impressions, and some investment in evaluation will be worthwhile in all cases.

The steps suggested for structuring a before-and-after design are simple. First, carefully define what the innovation involves and how it is to be put into practice. Secondly, decide in advance what will serve as evidence that attainment has improved or deteriorated. Thirdly, in the light of these criteria of success or failure, specify what is to be observed or tested. This observation or testing should preferably be applied to the situation 'before' as well as to the new. But if it has to be from memory it should still be based on clearly specified aspects of learning, behaviour and attainment in the old method, and on the new, as it is put into practice.

Step 1: Clarifying the Innovation

Work out in advance the important aims of the new approach and the way it is to be implemented. This need not be in the form of objectives defined in terms of measurable behaviour, but should approximate to the more relaxed statements introduced in Chapter 2. There should be a clear idea of what the children are expected to learn, and of how this will be achieved. Thus, the preparation for evaluation fits into its proper place in the planning of the organisation of knowledge. It may be possible to rank the objectives in order of importance so that attention can be concentrated where it is most important.

Step 2: Specifying What Will Count as Evidence

When there is a clear idea of priorities, the standards expected of the children should be considered. This may be thought through in terms of criteria to be satisfied or standards to be achieved. For example, it may be considered essential that children learn to recognise the span of time between the six projects in the year, to place them in the correct century and to know the number of centuries between them. On a before-and-after basis this can provide a crude but useful indicator of the success achieved. Some teachers might define what they would consider to be mastery of this concept of historical times. This would mean spelling out what is involved, and the level of attainment that would count as mastery. This could be translated into a target of a percentage of children achieving this level. Success is then related to a specified level of attainment. For evaluation to be useful there has to be a clear idea of the learning expected and the standards that should be achieved.

Step 3: Specify What is to be Observed or Tested

Once objectives and expected standards, however crude, have been specified, it is necessary to decide on ways of collecting evidence on the relevant attainments. In some cases the attainment may be important enough for a special test to be designed. The essential point is that the evidence to be used in comparing 'before' and 'after' should be based on observing or testing the same aspects. Like must be compared with like. Thus, there must be specification before the comparisons are made. Where there can only be recall of what went 'before', the specification will at least guide the memory, although the comparison will be suspect.

In a few cases it may be valid to use a standardised test for the comparison of performance. This is most likely in reading or mathematics. But the 'fit' of test to the objectives of the teaching must be close. The advantage of using standardised tests is that they provide a control group for the teacher. The scores on a conventional norm-referenced test are derived from a large sample of children on whom the test has been piloted during construction, and on which its norms are based. Thus, both 'before' and 'after' test scores are related to the scores of this third, 'control' group. There are, however, dangers in this method. The children in the year-group or class may differ in some important way when compared with the group used for constructing the standardised test, and this might invalidate the results. Secondly, the use of such tests promotes a false confidence in the results. There have been thousands of evaluations using standardised tests. Many have concluded with statistically significant results, yet later experience rarely bears out the confidence expressed in these results by the evaluators. Similarly, the rest of the evaluations, with non-significant results statistically, often turn out to be educationally very significant. It is often safer to rely on professional judgement and be wary, than to rest secure on the results of standardised tests that may not be fully reliable and valid, and may not be testing the aspects most dear to the teachers involved. Too many 'significant' results have turned out to be misleading for the gain in confidence from the use of standardised tests in quasi-experimental conditions to be recommended without caution.

Thus, the most common way of ensuring that the observations or tests before and after are comparable, is to spell out in advance what is to be in focus. Even if what went before is to be recalled rather than observed as it happens, there will be some comparability. Our teacher interested in the concept of historical time will have been looking for evidence that children can place important events in time, and relate them to others that were contemporaneous, earlier or later. She will have developed methods of assessing by asking questions, setting written work, organising and listening to discussions, watching the children at work and, occasionally, testing. A mix of these, chosen for their reliability and validity, can be tried out, improved and applied in the evaluation. The try-out or pilot is important. Only in practice can the bugs in the method be detected and ironed out.

Step 4: Collecting Background Information

Much energy has been used producing evaluations of major projects without anything very conclusive emerging. We still do not know how successful the Educational Priority Area action research following the Plowden Report was; and despite the massive investment involved, the evaluations of the US Head Start programme were inconclusive. The reason has often lain less in technical design than in failure to implement the programme. The evaluators were often looking for the results of something which in practice had never happened. The technical weaknesses in the before-and-after design are in reduced control. But control is no good if, in reality, there was nothing to evaluate. The crude comparison at least leaves time to fill in the background and to establish what has actually happened. Thus, formative evaluation can supplement the summative.

The advantages of this formative evaluation to the teacher are that it adds information which can be used to improve the way the learning is organised. Observations of the way the methods used before and after involve all children, affect their working habits, change the way the attention of the teacher is allocated, alter the way she operates and the impact on the remaining and related work of the children, are important background information that can illuminate an evaluation. The before-and-after design is suited to formative evaluation. It also frees time for it.

These four steps will help to add some reliability to the most common form of evaluation in the armoury of teachers. But control will still be lacking. There may be some point in time where the changed procedures or curriculum are so important that the control should not be sacrificed. If the formation of randomly allocated control groups is not possible, it might be feasible to give parallel classes the new method or content in different halves of the year, so that one half can serve as control for the other. Groups within a class can be treated in the same way. Another possibility is to arrange a class into groups and organise the programme so that each group gets its own variation. Here each group serves as a control on the rest. There are a variety of such designs and there are simple sources of technical advice on their use (see, for example, Fitz-Gibbon and Morris, 1978).

There is one extension to the before-and-after design that does not involve a control group, yet can bring greater confidence in any differences found. Instead of relying on a single set of observations or a single test before and after, these can be repeated. Hence the design becomes Figure 9.3.

Here the repeated observations or tests not only build up confidence, but provide points that can be graphed. Suppose our teacher of history has assessed her children's mastery of the concept of historical time before changing her teaching method, and then continues this assessment afterwards. The results, expressed as the percentage of children attaining mastery, may appear as figures on a graph, thus giving some confidence that there has been improvement, where a single assessment before and after would carry less credibility.

Figure 9.3: Before-and-after Design with Repeated Observations

(Observation, ↗(Observation,   (Innovation or↗(Observation, ↗(Observation,
 test, etc. 1)↗ test, etc. 2) etc experiment)↗ test, etc. 3)↗ test, etc. 4) etc.

In all these attempts to improve the reliability of evaluation designs, the importance of the priority to the organisation of learning, with evaluation forming a part of that process, has to be stressed. The choice of the crudest evaluation design to elaborate was not perversity, but a recognition that this is in continual use by teachers as they plan and look back on their work. Thus, the importance of maximising the use of professional judgements has also to be emphasised. Repeating the observations or tests is a way of strengthening your own judgements. Asking other teachers to add their judgements is another. In the end evidence in science is accepted because scientists agree among themselves that it is convincing. The conviction that the sun revolved around the earth was confirmed by evidence, and believed because that was the shared belief of all but a few heretics. More recently scientists believed that the atom was the smallest particle and that it could not be split. The evidence was believed because most believed it. Similarly, evidence on the best ways of organising learning is not absolute. It will vary over time, and the dominant view of the evidence will be that shared among most professionals. Teachers should not be embarrassed that they cannot collect hard evidence about the success of their work. Their professional judgement about what succeeds and fails is, in the end, what will determine the evidence accepted. This professional consensus undermined intelligence testing. Piagetian stages were accepted and used as a basis for planning curriculum, yet the evidence on these has since been similarly undermined (Shipman, 1981). Given the importance of collective professional judgement, the most valuable approach to evaluation by the teacher is to obtain second and third opinions wherever possible. That means involving others and sleeping on judgements before reviewing the evidence again. It means discussions and consultations among staff. In this way evaluation is secured as a part of the way learning is organised.

10 EVALUATION IN THE SCHOOL

The two parts of this book have been separated, yet it would be odd if the evaluation of pupils did not contribute to that of the school as an organisation. Equally, there would be no point in evaluating the school if this did not contribute to improvements in learning. Evaluation is a way of thinking about learning and its organisation. Hence the focus on models rather than techniques. The key to useful evaluation is to see it as an integral part of the way schools are organised, not as tests to be imposed.

The justification for this view was that observations of the way teachers go about their work in the classroom and judge the success of their school, show that evaluation is implicit in all their important activities. Thus, the book has made explicit the models that were already in the minds of teachers and of the sequences of activities already used for evaluation. The advantage of this approach is not only in helping teachers improve the reliability and validity of their evaluation, but in binding it into the organisation of learning.

The advantages of seeing evaluation as part of the organisation of learning have been spelled out in both parts of the book. Curriculum planning, teaching methods and school management continue to have priority. Evaluation supports the planning and improvement. The emphasis on formative evaluation shortens the time between teaching, evaluation and feedback, so that pupils and teachers receive information on their strengths and weaknesses in time to do something about it. Learning is organised first, with evaluation second, so that it remains as a means to an end and not an end in itself.

Similar advantages accrue when this pragmatic approach to evaluation is applied to the school as an organisation. The form of evaluation is determined by the way the school is organised rather than being imposed on it. The common feature throughout is the merging of evaluation with organisation, whether of learning in the classroom or of planning for the school. It is not a technique to be applied, but sensitivity to evidence that is continually being collected, discussed and acted upon. Once that evidence is organised as suggested earlier, evaluation becomes a part of the picture of pupils' learning or of school organisation that all teachers carry round with them.

The example that follows is of a school that would not claim to be particularly interested in evaluation. It had been organised through a series of small steps that were responses to developments such as the ending of secondary selection and the tests that accompanied it. Neither was the school known to be exceptionally progressive. Like most primary schools it had abandoned streaming and moved to mixed-ability grouping in the early 1970s. Across that decade staff placed increased emphasis on individualised learning. This was seen to rest on keeping careful records of individual progress as part of the design of a curriculum that would enable children to move at different speeds and cover work of different breadth. But the priority to the basic, vehicle areas of language and mathematics remained.

By the mid-1970s the ending of selection for secondary schooling enabled the move to individualised learning to accelerate. By 1980 most time was spent on language and mathematics as a core, with integrated studies, including science, taking up about one third of the remaining timetable. Much of this basic and integrated work was individualised using materials produced within the school. The one unusual feature of the curriculum was timetabled study skills wherein children were taught to use reference books and materials, find sources and resources, use common scientific instruments, mathematical, and scientific concepts, search out and interpret local historical evidence, and to use simple geographical techniques.

The commitment to evaluation grew out of the need to keep careful records of the progress of individual children. It was increased by LEA publications on basic curriculum areas which stressed aspects which most children should master at specified ages. The LEA also encouraged voluntary school self-evaluation through the production of a booklet of questions for staff. By 1982 the staff had planned to give parents information that would meet the requirements of the 1980 Education Act and to provide clear reports on the way their children were progressing. Headteacher, deputy and staff accepted evaluation as a part of the learning package they were developing. One member of staff had attended an in-service course and produced assessment material as an assignment.

The headteacher took overall responsibility and specific responsibility for organising the evaluation of the school by the staff. The head also took responsibility for organising assessment in the language area. The deputy head took responsibility for organising pupil evaluation as a whole. Mathematics assessment was organised by a post-holder with responsibility in that area. Each class teacher was responsible for maintaining records on individual children, for relating these to the planning of work and for passing on the information to the deputy headteacher. The deputy received the information and compiled a central record of the progress for each pupil. Information on progress was collected in early November and at the end of the spring term. These were followed in early December and early summer term by discussions between the deputy head and teachers to ensure that the work of individual children was discussed and cases identified where action was necessary. At these meetings the deputy went through his records, and all teachers concerned contributed to discussions of individual children. In addition, there were another series of case conferences in late September to check progress at the start of the year. These were informal occasions, but the records kept ensured that the progress of all children was scrutinised.

School evaluation was organised by the headteacher at meetings of staff to review how things were going, and a pattern of one meeting per term had emerged. At first these were informal, under the direction of the head, and concerned with a scan of problems and progress. However, as developments in curriculum and organisation were being considered, the headteacher had asked particular teachers to work together to prepare a review or a plan for discussion. An LEA document on school self-assessment had focused this activity, and particular attention had been paid to the teaching of science as a result of the interest of the local advisory service.

This developing evaluation of the school as an organisation was being concentrated on critical aspects that could be managed in a situation of falling rolls and where capitation was being cut. While some of this was short-term planning to cope with the loss of a member of staff or to decide where the available money for new books should be allocated, some of it was longer term. The headteacher had moved towards reviewing the management of the school along the lines recommended by Jones (1980). Jones was writing about the management of primary schools and identified five key areas for attention and evaluation. These were curriculum, quality of teaching, allocation of capitation, buildings and communication.

The Evaluation of the Teaching of Language

The headteacher had designed four instruments for teachers to use in the organisation of the language curriculum. The first of these was a checklist for teachers of younger children to detect early language strengths and weaknesses. Much of this was concerned with the use of reading materials, word recognition and the early stages of writing. But there were also items on perceptual abilities, speech fluency and the capacity to listen and understand. It was stressed that this checklist was a way of helping teachers to detect strengths and weaknesses, not a replacement for professional judgement.

The second set of records was a folder for each child. In this was a record of books read. The child also selected what he or she thought to be the best of their written work during the year. This folder was taken home at the end of the year, and among top juniors served as a basis for a folder of work for the receiving secondary school at transfer. The headteacher saw most of the children during the year, and the folder formed the basis of the discussion. The aim was to enable the head-teacher to add a second opinion in specific cases.

The third instrument was a cumulative record for older children in the form of profiles for reading, writing and listening skills. In each of these there were series of skills listed with 'strong', 'moderate' and 'weak' as responses. They were filled up twice a year. Under the profiles was room for comment by the teacher on progress made since the last assessment and the steps taken to produce this. These records were completed by the class teacher and handed in to the headteacher. The head then saw individual cases where there was an obvious difficulty, and used the record if a child was being interviewed as part of the programme of double-checking individual progress. The records were returned to the class teacher with comments. They were also used in case conferences on children organised by the deputy headteacher.

The fourth record was a simple checklist for the teachers in all years to help them keep a check on progress through the language curriculum. The skills listed were the same as those used in the individual profiles, but here the progress of all the children was recorded with a tick. The objective was not to check mastery of the skills in reading, writing, speaking and listening in any accurate way, but to give the teacher an easily produced picture of progress by all the children in the class so that the work could be planned with continuity, and paced so that the slow were not left behind and the quick not bored. This checklist also served as an outline syllabus. It was used as a loose guide, allowing teachers to alter breadth, depth and speed according to the work done in previous years. It also allowed for individuality of approach by teachers, while guaranteeing that there would be a minimum of structure whatever approach was used.

This rather elaborate evaluation of the elements in the language curriculum meant that at any one time a teacher had to maintain two records. The first was either the screening record for younger children or the cumulative record for older juniors; the second was the teacher's own record of progress. In addition, each teacher had to keep an eye on the folder of work kept by all children. This was felt to be excessive, and changes had been discussed with the headteacher at one of the meetings on school evaluation. The teachers also had to organise the LEA screening test at the end of the infant stage and another standardised test for the LEA for the top juniors.

Evaluation of the Teaching of Mathematics

Mathematics in the school had been influenced by the efforts of the LEA advisory staff to get agreement on a core of common mathematics in junior schools to solve the problems faced by secondary teachers receiving pupils at 11 from a large number of schools with different syllabuses. As the in-service work to raise the level of mathematical skills available was organised, the LEA tried to ensure that each school had a post-holder who could take responsibility for the mathematics curriculum. There was no single method of evaluation in mathematics recommended, but the in-service courses had contained sessions where suggestions for the use of checklists had been made.

The mathematics post-holder had introduced a single and simple checklist for each child that would also serve as a progress chart for the teacher. An extract follows. There were four parts in the mathematics syllabus: 'Sets', 'Numbers', 'Measures' and 'Geometry'. Each was divided into sections. Thus, the 'Numbers' part consisted of 'Whole Numbers', 'Operations with Whole Numbers', 'Patterns and Properties of Whole Numbers', 'Fractional Numbers' and 'Statistics involving Counts'. These sections were then sub-divided into specific skills. Here is an extract from the mathematics progress record selected from part of the 'Numbers' section:

	Concept/skill experienced	Initial understanding	Fully understood
Inequalities and concrete subtraction activities			

Subtraction using
numbers to 10

Subtracting numbers to
10 from numbers 10
to 20

Subtraction of tens
and units using decom-
position

This record was filled in with a tick when the child started on the
activities, was beginning to get a grasp of the idea, and when the concept
or skill had been mastered. While this was an individual record to plot
pupil progress, it covered the mathematics syllabus through the school.
Teachers could get a guide to the progress of a class while children
were working individually, by looking at a particular concept and
observing how many children were just starting, in the middle of the
work, or had finished. The record had been designed to support the
way mathematics had been organised, and was reproduced on sheets
that could be handed on with the child at the end of the year or when
he or she left.

Teachers used this record with various degrees of enthusiasm. Some
filled it in as they observed children working, collected answer sheets for
marking and comments, and backed up their judgement with class tests.
Others used ticks on an impressionistic basis. Thus, there was some doubt
about the commitment to the schedule, but there was no doubt that it was
a powerful reinforcement for the mathematics curriculum. Children were
supposed to progress through the work scheduled and teachers were tick-
ing that this was proceeding. The scheme was being amended as discussions over evaluation took place under the guidance of the deputy head.

The Evaluation of Study Skills

Part of the programme of integrated studies was a planned series of
exercises to develop study skills. This was a pragmatic exercise, seen as
a way of improving performance in every aspect of work and preparing children for individual work. This was an excellent example of
the way useful evaluation follows and feeds the planning of learning.
The skills were seen as essential, exercises were worked out to ensure
that children would learn them, and evaluation was added to check that

they had been completed.

Each child kept a record sheet containing a list of the exercises to be completed. At the end of each exercise the child ticked the relevant box and added the date. The record was then taken to the teacher who initialled it, discussed the exercise with the child, and added a comment or instruction for further work in a space provided. The next exercise was then started. The record was kept by the child in a folder along with the completed worksheets in each exercise. Some of the exercises were to be completed at home, and the children were encouraged to take the folder home and to involve their parents.

An example of the exercises was use of the local reference library. Children were set an exercise that took them to the library to look up information and use it to answer a series of questions. In this case the initials of the librarian were required as the child completed the work. These were simple exercises that most children would be engaged in without help from teachers. But the programme ensured that children had exercised the skills and could benefit from other work in the school that used them.

There was no deliberate attempt to link pupil to school evaluation. However, the development of evaluation to ensure that the progress of all children was monitored and discussed, and the care taken to use the information gained to alter the way learning was organised, had secured a central place for evaluation in the way staff managed their work. The evidence was not hidden away in records, but used in regular discussions about children. This became especially important when they were about to move to secondary school and information for the transfer was being prepared. The regular case conferences and the careful use of evaluation to ensure that children tracked through the curriculum without discontinuity had a further beneficial effect. The evaluation itself was under continual review, as it had to serve a useful purpose in planning and in the organisation of help for pupils, or be criticised itself. In this sense the incomplete organisation of evaluation was an advantage. Nothing was made routine and in danger of becoming redundant.

Finally, the emphasis on evaluation for use was helpful as the staff planned to increase the information for parents following the 1980 Education Act. The school prospectus, the newsletters and parents' meetings were re-organised along with reports on individual children. The aim was to involve parents in thinking and action about their children and about the curriculum of the school. This concern with external relations was given priority as a school-based, self-evaluation exercise.

It would be convenient to ignore the shortcomings in the evaluation exercise in this school and to play down the objections to the time it took. Some teachers thought it had been given too high a priority and took energy that would have been better spent in teaching. But the discussions at every stage had involved them, and hostile or not, it was impossible to ignore the importance given to evaluation in the school. It had succeeded in converting the impressions and staffroom gossip into better informed judgements. The emphasis on evaluation had created a climate in which evaluation was being improved and not seen as threatening.

Levels of Evaluation

The evaluation just described was on its way to being an integral part of the organisation of learning and of management in the school. Inevitably, the commitment of staff differed. More importantly, the level at which evaluation was conducted had not been settled. To most teachers the evidence was useful as a source for checking how well their teaching was going and for planning future work. For a few, evaluation remained an appendage, useful for overcoming problems, whether these arose in school organisation or for an individual pupil or class. At the other extreme evaluation was accepted as a way of confirming that the curriculum and school organisation were problematic. The majority accepted that evaluation was a part of school management. They saw that it arose out of the way work was planned. But this acceptance still left staff involved in using evaluation for very different reasons. Inevitably this led to misunderstandings. Evaluation serves very different purposes, as described in Chapter 1. Even when staff carry around a similar model of the place of evaluation in the working of the school, they may still be looking for evidence to use in very different ways. Four levels where evaluation is used can be separated: problem-solving, maintenance, system-management and research. At each of these levels the six purposes of evaluation, diagnosis, guidance, selection, prediction and judgement may be given priority. These levels can be found in pupil as well as in school evaluation. An excellent account of these activities for accountability purposes can be found in Becher, Eraut and Knight (1981).

Problem-solving

Teachers are natural trouble-shooters. The school day is filled with judgements of behaviour that serve for instantaneous action to defuse, remedy or avoid problems. In many schools evaluation is confined to this trouble-shooting function. Staff spot a problem, rapidly collect evidence to evaluate the causes and then act to overcome it. It can be unrelated to the way learning or the school is organised. In this sense it is expedient, and need be of little lasting value. Yet it is an essential activity among teachers, and the anticipation of problems is helped by an awareness of clues and cues.

Problem-solving evaluation can also be made routine rather than remain one-off problem-spotting. Staff can be organised to ensure that the work of the school is under continuing observation. Once again this is normal procedure. Teachers scan the walls, look into the toilets, watch the children as they leave school, listen for the noise in the dining room, and pay careful attention to behaviour in corridors. In the classroom they watch for signs of boredom, of disruption or distraction. They watch children for signs of understanding, frustration or enthusiasm. They may formalise this by routine checks on exercise books, by calling out selected children to look at their work, by moving around the class to see how the work is progressing.

Maintenance

Schools build indicators into their management. The basic school record is often organised so that norm-referenced indicators of standards in language and mathematics can be checked annually. There are meetings of staff to discuss the progress of individual children and of groups. The continuity and the relationships within the curriculum are reviewed. There are arrangements for ensuring that parents are kept informed of the progress of their own children and of developments within the school. Attendance, accidents, punishments are recorded. Each record serves to indicate the state of play in some aspect of school organisation.

These maintenance arrangements take the form of quality control. In the example described earlier, the headteacher had taken responsibility for the language curriculum, and there was a post-holder responsible for advising on mathematics and science throughout the school. These areas of the curriculum were being reviewed and developed, not only by internal discussion but by bringing in ideas obtained from in-service courses and LEA advisors. Curriculum renewal was being secured by regular monitoring, using questions asked as part of routine discussions about the way learning was organised.

System-management

The arrangements for maintenance in the example used earlier covered separate aspects of school organisation. They were being organised as resources became available. There was, however, little that related these arrangements to the priorities stressed in the prospectus of the school. The headteacher was clear in stating the aims of the school, but there was no model that related these to the developing monitoring of the working of the school. Yet many schools have moved in this direction, laying out what the school stands for and then specifying the standards that are expected to be attained. Examples can be found in Chapter 6.

The aims, objectives, organisation, evaluation, feedback sequence has a rationality about it that is attractive. It provides a model that enables the management of particular aspects to be referred to the aims that are supposed to be achieved, thus making it easier to decide on priorities for action in a rational manner. Above all, the emphasis on feedback from evaluation promises to minimise redundancy in the organisation. There are, however, objections to this model when applied to schools. They are not mechanistic, and aims might be achieved in ways that cannot be evaluated systematically. Indeed, some priorities, for example in the pastoral area, might be undermined by evaluation. Further, the importance of external factors can result in misleading or incomplete feedback if social background and other influences are not taken into account.

Research

Organising evaluation for solving problems as they arise, or for maintaining the efficiency of the organisation, or as an integral part of the model for the school are useful management devices. They are implicit in all schools, whether applied to the organisation of learning or to the management of the school. They all involve evaluation to monitor the organisation. But they also share an approach that takes that organisation as given. The problems that are identified and solved, the routines that are maintained, the system that is monitored, are all influenced by the evaluation. But that evaluation is a means of making the existing arrangements more effective. It is not used as a way of asking new questions about them.

Much research tackles problems that are identified in the management of services such as education. Curriculum evaluation, for example, is usually concerned with the effects of introducing new, or changing existing courses. The course and the way it is taught is accepted as given. Researchers, however, including curriculum evaluators, also adopt an open-ended approach in which the subject of their interest is seen as problematic, open to question. Here the outcome is not confined to producing evidence of use in managing school or classroom, but can throw light not only on the way things are organised, but the assumptions behind that organisation.

This probing approach is not clearly separated from one that just informs management. Evaluation is judgement. A teacher may test the learning of long division, but is also likely to question whether it is a worthwhile exercise in the days of cheap calculators. A head-teacher may decide on spot checks on attendance to ensure that there is no registering and then slipping away, but is also likely to ask why this seems to be a possible problem, or indeed, whose problem it is. This research approach is uncomfortable because it is open-ended and the results are unpredictable. Hypotheses are not only tested but sought. These may produce subversive ideas that schools actually produce their own truancy rates or build failure into identifiable groups of children. But even the conventional hypothesis-testing approach may produce challenging evidence. Many evaluations of new developments conclude with results that show no statistically significant differences between the new and the existing arrangements. That is disappointing to those who are enthusiastic about the new. But it leaves questions for the researcher and for the audience for the evidence. The development may be educationally very significant; but even if it is not, there is the follow-up question about why the research failed to detect the expected differences. At that point the focus is liable to shift to asking questions about the innovation itself and the assumptions, not only of those who introduced it, but of those who designed the research. All research is potentially subversive in the useful way of probing below the way things are organised to the underlying assumptions.

When this research is adopted in schools it can be combined with action in a profitable way, raising the awareness of teachers. In books reporting studies by 'teachers as researchers' (Nixon, 1981 and Eggleston, 1980) there are case studies of classrooms, school organisation and of support services around the school. The Ford Teaching Project (Elliott, 1978) was organised to examine ways of implementing enquiry-based methods across the curriculum. John Elliott, who directed the Ford Teaching Project, was also the director of the Cambridge Accountability Project (Cambridge Institute of Education, 1981) in which teachers produced extensive case studies of developments in their schools. In all these cases teacher-based research was a way of reflecting upon schooling within a specific context, and acting upon the findings.

The published accounts of research by teachers in their schools are a small proportion of the total activity. The journal *School Organisation* contains many other examples. Many initiatives remain unpublished. In reality, like evaluation, research merges into the everyday activity of teachers. It is less the application of pre-determined techniques than a systematic approach to important issues in the school. Nixon (1981, pp. 5–6) puts it this way:

> Action research is an intellectually demanding mode of enquiry, which prompts serious and often uncomfortable questions about classroom practice. It requires a willingness on the part of teachers to learn about their own classrooms and a desire to develop themselves professionally. The teacher who engages in action research is not a special kind of teacher, but simply one who wishes to increase his or her professional expertise.

As with all the evaluation discussed in this book, it is possible to find all four of the levels above in most schools. Teachers not only keep their eyes open for incipient problems, select important aspects from which indicators can be routinely observed, feed back evidence to adjust ends and means, but test out and generate hunches about the reasons behind problems, routines and organisation. An excellent example was the challenge to the use of intelligence tests. The scepticism among teachers preceded that among academics. The sceptics in the classroom not only challenged the results for individual children, the average for the class, the validity as assessed by the match between their assessment and that yielded by the test, they queried the reasoning behind the test content and construction. To many teachers the idea of intelligence fixed early in life and not open to learning seemed absurd. Their own evidence on children who failed the 11 plus and then obtained good O and A levels in a secondary modern school confirmed their suspicions. Teachers do not just accept definitions, concepts, theories and categories. They make their own problems and investigate them. That too is evaluation.

The most useful balance for a school would be readiness to spot problems and look for answers, to organise routine evaluations to feed into classroom and school management, with some more probing action research. This is often possible because a member of staff is on a course or taking a qualification where such research is required. But it is also a way of ensuring that problems are identified in good time, that injustices are detected, and that the staff are involved in the excitement of uncovering the gaps between what is supposed to be happening and what is actually going on.

The Use of Existing Evidence

Throughout this book there has been reference to the difficulty in obtaining relevant external evidence against which the performance within the school can be compared. The technical difficulty where this involves standards of individual attainment makes it highly likely that any comparisons will be dubious. There is less of a problem when the external data are about the curriculum, the balance of subjects, topics within them, the time allocated to each, the relative performance of different groups, the relation between teaching styles, and the way children are organised to learn. Here there is evidence in plenty from surveys on how schools are organised, the variety of curricula and the performance of girls and boys, blacks and whites, white and blue-collar workers' children and so on. Here the questions are not about products but processes. References containing useful data can be found in Appendix 1.

There is, however, another and more comprehensive reason for organising the information available from published evaluations, research and descriptive surveys. It provides both the evidence for alerting staff to what is going on nationally or locally, and material to guide evaluations within the school. The Southgate, Arnold and Johnson (1981) study *Extending Beginning Reading* provides an important example. There is some evidence on standards. For example, only one-fifth of average readers aged 8 in the survey were able to read all the 200 most commonly used words in the English language. It gives a lot of information on weaknesses in reading. But even more important, it contains evidence on the way reading is organised for the 7 to 9 year olds, and suggests that in most cases this was not effective and, because of the logistics of the classroom, could not be so. That is a useful start for a review of the way language is taught in school. It is made more urgent by the evidence that teachers did not seem to identify the weaknesses of children through the methods used, although these were individualised.

There are many research reports from academics, from the Schools Council, from the National Foundation for Educational Research, from HM Inspectorate, from the Department of Education and Science, from the Assessment of Performance Unit, from committees and commissions, as well as from international bodies such as the Organisation for Economic Co-operation and Development (OECD) that provide a wealth of material for the start of evaluation within the school. These are not examples to be copied, but evidence against which the organisation of learning in the school can be compared. They are a starter for evaluation, yielding data against which staff can question their own arrangements.

All APU reports on mathematics, English and science contain scores on written and often on practical tests. They also contain examples of questions, and of scores attained on them. But there are difficulties in using these for comparisons with children in a particular school. APU testing is designed to obtain national data, and the curriculum in any one school or even any one LEA is unlikely to match that sampled by the tests. That is deliberate policy, and the sample is fixed so that LEAs and schools cannot be identified. Hence, it would be misleading for any one school to use sample questions, or tables of average scores for comparison. The school may have a curriculum that is very different from that sampled in the surveys. Thus APU survey results are useful for national assessment, but do not provide standards against which individual school performance can be measured.

Perhaps the most useful information for individual schools that can be derived from APU and other published test results, is the identification of aspects of language or mathematics or science where national performance is strong or weak. The three surveys of mathematics attainment among 11-year-olds, for example, have indicated a sound knowledge of basic mathematics skills, but weaknesses when these are applied in problems and practical situations. This is valuable information for teachers in alerting them to aspects where attention might usefully be given. For example, the first science survey of 11-year-olds (DES, 1981, pp. 95-104, 175) tested 'making sense of information using science concepts'. Sample questions out of the 42 used are reported with results. The 1,100 children involved were asked to go beyond recall to apply the concepts covered by the tests. The results reflected learning through engaging in science activities, rather than picked up without teaching. Here the distribution of marks tended to be U-shaped, with the right-hand arm missing because of reduced frequency with increasing scores. This weakness is using scientific concepts has to be treated with caution, but has important implications for science in the junior school if confirmed by later surveys of the same age group. On this aspect 'striking' differences were reported between scores of boys and girls (DES, 1981, pp. 102-3). In the more general aspects tested, girls were ahead of the boys. But in the more science-specific aspects such as the application of scientific concepts, boys were ahead of the girls.

Again it is necessary to urge caution in using APU, or any research evidence. It should be used as setting problems for teachers, alerting them to areas of their work where attention is needed and as a source of suggestions for developments. Research evidence is a supplement, not a replacement for professional judgement. It is often a challenge to existing practices, rarely a blueprint for immediate action. But that is also the message throughout this book.

There is no clear divide between quantitative assessment and qualitative evaluation. The former may involve standardised procedures and produce numerical indicators of performance, but these are shot through with the professional assumptions of the designers. Furthermore, when they are used by teachers the scores are interpreted before action is taken. This is normal professional practice. A dentist X-rays your teeth, but then judges where to drill or pull. A doctor checks your pulse, but makes up his mind only after considering all the symptoms, your medical history and your own description of the old complaint. If necessary he asks for a second opinion. This book is an invitation to evaluation. Thus, it is also more concerned with second opinions and improving judgements than with testing. It is a guide to professional action, not a substitute for it.

APPENDIX: USEFUL REFERENCES

General Books on Assessment

Black, H.D. and Broadfoot, P.M. (1982) *Keeping Track of Teaching*, Routledge & Kegan Paul
Broadfoot, P.M. (1979) *Assessment, Schools and Society*, Methuen
Harlen, W. (ed.) (1978) *Evaluation and the Teacher's Role*, Macmillan
Open University (1982) *Curriculum Assessment and Evaluation in Educational Institutions*, E364, Open University
Rowntree, D. (1977) *Assessing Students. How Shall we Know Them?*, Harper & Row
Satterley, D. (1981) *Assessment in Schools*, Blackwell
Sumner, R. and Bradley, K. (1979) *Assessment for Transition: A Study of New Procedures*, National Foundation for Educational Research

Records and Recording

Clift, P., Weiner, G. and Wilson, E. (1981) *Record-keeping in the Primary School*, Macmillan
Cooper, K. (1976) *Assessment and Record Keeping in History, Geography and Social Science*, Collins/Schools Council
Foster, J. (1971) *Recording Individual Progress*, Macmillan
Hodges, L. (1981) *The School Records Debate*, Writers & Readers Publishing Cooperative

Self-evaluation in Schools

Burgess, T. and Adams, E. (eds.) (1980) *Outcomes of Education*, Macmillan
Davis, E. (1981) *Teachers as Curriculum Evaluators*, Allen & Unwin
Eggleston, S.J. (ed.) (1980) *School-based Curriculum Development in Britain*, Routledge & Kegan Paul
Elliott, G. (1980) *Self Evaluation and the Teacher*, University of Hull
McCormick, R. (ed.) (1981) *Calling Education to Account*, Heinemann
Nixon, J. (1981) *A Teachers' Guide to Action Research*, Grant McIntyre

157

158   *Appendix: Useful References*

Schools Council (1981) *The Practical Curriculum*, Methuen
Shipman, M.D. (1979) *In-school Evaluation*, Heinemann
Simons, H. (1979) 'The Evaluative School', *Forum*, vol. 22

Local Education Authority Self-evaluation Documents

Birmingham (1980) *Self-assessment within Primary Schools*
Clwyd (1980) *School Self-evaluation: a Discussion Paper*
ILEA (1977) *Keeping the School Under Review*
Lancashire (1980) *A Schedule of Self-appraisal*
Oxfordshire (1979) *Starting Points in Self-evaluation*
Solihull (1979) *Evaluating the School: a Guide for Secondary Schools*
Solihull (1980) *Evaluating the Primary School*

Sources of Useful Information for Comparison

Assessment of Performance Unit (APU) (1980) *Mathematical Development, Primary School Survey 1*, HMSO
―― (1981) *Mathematical Development, Primary School Survey 2*, HMSO
―― (1982) *Mathematical Development, Primary School Survey 3*, HMSO
―― (1981) *Language Performance in Schools, Primary School Report 1*, HMSO
―― (1982) *Language Performance in Schools, Primary School Report 2*, HMSO
―― (1981) *Science in Schools, Age 11: Report No. 1*, HMSO
Bassey, M. (1977) *Nine Hundred Primary School Teachers*, Trent Polytechnic
Bennett, S.N. (1976) *Teaching Styles and Pupil Progress*, Basic Books
Bennett, S.N. *et al.* (1980) *Open Plan Schools*, National Foundation for Educational Research, for the Schools Council
Boydell, D. (1981) 'Classroom Organisation', in B. Simon and J. Willcocks (eds.) *Research and Practice in the Primary Classroom*, Routledge & Kegan Paul, pp. 36–42
Equal Opportunities Commission, (1982) *Do You Provide Equal Educational Opportunities?*, Equal Opportunities Commission
Galton, M., Simon, B. and Croll, P. (1980) *Inside the Primary Classroom*, Routledge & Kegan Paul

Galton, M. and Simon, B. (1980) *Progress and Performance in the Primary Classroom*, Routledge & Kegan Paul
Southgate, V., Arnold, H. and Johnson, S. (1981) *Extending Beginning Reading*, Heinemann

Department of Education and Science (DES) Reports

DES (1978) *Primary Education in England*, HMSO
―― (1980) *A View of the Curriculum*, HMSO
―― (1981) *The School Curriculum*, HMSO
―― (1982) *Education 5 to 9*, HMSO

Accountability

Becker, T., Eraut, M. and Knight, J. (1981) *Policies for Educational Accountability*, Heinemann
Cambridge Accountability Project (1981) *Case Studies in School Accountability*, Cambridge Institute of Education
Lello, J. (1979) *Accountability in Education*, Ward Lock

BIBLIOGRAPHY

Ashton, P. (1975) *The Aims of Primary Education*, Macmillan, London
Assessment of Performance Unit (1981) *Science in Schools; Age 11, Report No. 1*, HMSO, London
Bastiani, J. (1978) *Written Communication between Home and School*, University of Nottingham School of Education, Nottingham
Becher, T., Eraut, M. and Knight, J. (1981) *Policies for Educational Accountability*, Heinemann, London
Bennett, S.N. *et al.* (1980) *Open Plan Schools*, NFER, Windsor
Black, H.D. and Dockrell, W.B. (1980) *Diagnostic Assessment*, SCRE, Edinburgh
Bloom, B.S. (1956) *Taxonomy of Educational Objectives: Cognitive Domain*, Longman, London
Blyth,W.A.L. *et al.* (1976) *Place, Time and Society*, Collins-ESL, Bristol
Boydell, D. (1981) 'Classroom Organisation 1970-77', in B. Simon and J. Willcocks (eds.), *Research and Practice in the Primary Classroom*, Routledge & Kegan Paul, London, 36-42
Bristol, University of (1982) *Guidelines for Review and Institutional Development in Schools (GRIDS)*, Bristol
Bruce, J. (1981) 'Match', *School Organisation*, 1, 1, pp. 53-65
Bullock Report (1975) *A Language for Life* (Report of the Committee of Inquiry), HMSO, London
Cambridge Institute of Education (1981) *Case Studies in School Accountability*, Cambridge
Cheshire Education Committee (1981) *Curriculum 11-16, Cheshire Reappraisal Group*, Chester
Clark, T. (1981) 'Coherent Curriculum through Staff Development', *School Organisation*, 1, 3, pp. 325-42
Clift, P. (1979) 'Parental Involvement in Primary Schools: The NFER Survey', mimeographed paper. See also Cyster, R. and Clift, P. (1980), 'Parental Involvement in Primary Schools: The NFER Survey', in Craft, M. *et al.*, *Linking Home and School*, Harper & Row, London, pp. 152-64
Clift, P., Weiner, G. and Wilson, E. (1981) *Record Keeping in the Primary School*, Macmillan, London
Commission for Racial Equality (1976) *Education for a Multicultural Society: A Bibliography for Teachers*, CRE, London

Cooper, K. (1976) *Evaluation, Assessment and Record Keeping in History, Geography and Social Science*, Collins/Schools Council, London

Daniels, J.C. and Diack, H. (1958) *The Standard Reading Test*, Chatto Educational, London

Davies, E. (1980) 'Primary School Records' in Burgess, T. and Adams, E., *Outcomes of Education*, Macmillan, London, pp. 122-31

Department of Education and Science (DES) (1977) *Curriculum 11-16*, HMSO, London, see also DES (1981) *Curriculum 11-16: A Review of Progress*, HMSO, London

—— (1978) *Primary Education in England*, HMSO, London

—— (1980a) *A Framework for the School Curriculum*, HMSO, London

—— (1980b) *A View of the Curriculum*, HMSO, London

—— (1981) *The School Curriculum*, HMSO, London

—— (1982) *Education 5 to 9*, HMSO, London

Douglas, J.W.B. (1964) *The Home and the School*, MacGibbon & Kee, London

Eggleston, S.J. (ed.) (1980) *School-based Curriculum Development in Britain*, Routledge & Kegan Paul, London

Elliott, G. (1981) *Self-evaluation and the Teacher*, University of Hull, Hull

Elliott, J. (1978) 'Classroom Accountability and the Self-monitoring Teacher' in W. Harlen (ed.), *Evaluation and the Teachers' Role*, Macmillan, London

Elliott, J. (1982) 'Some Key Concepts Underlying Teachers' Evaluations of Innovations', in Open University, E204, *Purpose and Planning in the Curriculum*, Unit 26, Block 4

Fitz-Gibbon, C.T. and Morris, L.L. (1978) *How to Design a Program Evaluation*, Sage Publications, London

Foster, J. (1971) *Recording Individual Progress*, Macmillan, London

Frisby, C. (1982) 'Records and Assessment', *Forum*, 24, 2, pp. 37-9

Galton, M. and Simon, B. (1980) *Progress and Performance in the Primary Classroom*, Routledge & Kegan Paul, London

Gates-MacGinitie (1972) *Reading Test*, NFER, Windsor

Get Reading Right Test (1971), Gibson, Glasgow

Glasman, N.S. and Biniaminov, I. (1981) 'Input-Output Analyses of Schools', *Review of Educational Research*, 51, 4, pp. 509-39

Hadow Report (1931) *Report of the Consultative Committee on The Primary School*, HMSO, London

Hamilton, D. (1976) *Curriculum Evaluation*, Open Books, London

Harlen, W. (1977) *Match and Mismatch*, Oliver and Boyd, Edinburgh

162   *Bibliography*

Harrison, A. (1982) *A Review of Graded Tests*, Methuen, London

Hawkins, P. (1973) *An Observation Procedure for Use in Schools*, Inner London Education Authority, London

Hicks, D.W. (1981) *Minorities*, Heinemann, London

Hirst, P.H. (1974) *Knowledge and the Curriculum*, Routledge & Kegan Paul, London

Hodges, L. (1981) *Out in the Open? The School Records Debate*, Writers and Readers Publishing Cooperative, London

Inner London Education Authority (ILEA) (undated) *Music Guidelines*, ILEA, London

—— (1977) *Keeping the School Under Review*, ILEA, London

—— (1978) *Primary School Mathematics 2: Checkpoints*, ILEA, London

—— (1979) *The London Reading Test*, NFER, Windsor

—— (1980) *Social Studies in the Primary School*, ILEA, London

Institute for Personality and Ability Testing (1973) *Measuring Intelligence with the CULTURE FAIR TEST*, IPAT, Illinois

Jackson, P.M. and Belford, E. (1965) 'Private Affairs in Public Settings: Observations on Teaching in Elementary Schools', *School Review*, Summer, pp. 172–86

Johnson, D. and Ransom, E. (1980) 'Parents' Perceptions of Secondary Schools', in M. Craft, J. Raynor and L. Cohen (eds.), *Linking Home and School*, Harper & Row, London, pp. 177–85

Jones, R. (1980) *Primary School Management*, David & Charles, London

Kratwohl, D.R. (1964) *Taxonomy of Educational Objectives: The Affective Domain*, Longman, London

Leith, S. (1981) 'Project Work' in B. Simon and J. Willcocks (eds.) *Research and Practice in the Primary Classroom*, Routledge & Kegan Paul, London, pp. 55–64

Little, A. and Willey, R. (1981) *Multi-ethnic Education. The Way Forward*, Schools Council, London

McIntosh, H.G. and Hale, D.E. (1976) *Assessment and the Secondary School Teacher*, Routledge & Kegan Paul, London

Marshall, C.P. and Wolfendale, S. (1977) 'Screening and Early Identification of Children with Problems' in J. Galliband (ed.), *Reading: Research and Classroom Practice*, Ward Lock, London, pp. 228–37

Neal, P.D. (1975) *Continuity in Education (EDC Project 5)*, Birmingham Education Committee, Birmingham

Newton, M.J. and Thomson, M.W. (1976) *The Aston Index*, Learning Development Aids, Wisbech

Nixon, J. (1981) *A Teachers' Guide to Action Research*, Grant McIntyre, London

Nuffield Foundation (1972) *Checking Up, 1, 11 & 111,* Chambers, Edinburgh

Open University (1982a) *Curriculum Evaluation and Assessment in Educational Institutions,* E364, Open University, Milton Keynes

Open University (1982b) *Curriculum in Action,* Open University, Milton Keynes

Oxfordshire Education Committee (1979) *Starting Points in Self-evaluation,* Oxford

Plowden Report (1976) *Children and Their Primary Schools,* HMSO, London

Prosser, M. (1982) 'Heads Get Staff Support in Self-evaluation', *Times Educational Supplement,* 18.6.1982, p. 12.

Reynell Development Language Scales (1969), NFER, Windsor

Reynolds, J. and Skilbeck, M. (1976) *Culture and the Classroom,* Open Books, London

Sale, L.L. (1979) *Introduction to Middle School Teaching,* C.A. Merrill, New York

Salford Education Department (1977) *The Primary School Profile,* Salford

Satterley, D. (1981) *Assessment in Schools,* Blackwell, Oxford

Schonell, F. (1945) *The Psychology and Teaching of Reading,* Oliver & Boyd, London

School of Oriental and African Studies (1978) *Africa: A Teachers' Handbook,* SOAS, London

Schools Council (1970) *Initial Literacy Project (Breakthrough to Literacy),* Longman, London

—— (1981a) *The Practical Curriculum,* Methuen, London

—— (1981b) *Education for a Multiracial Society,* Schools Council, London

Scottish Council for Research in Education (1977) *Pupils in Profile,* Hodder & Stoughton, London

Shipman, M.D. (1981) *The Limitations of Social Research,* 2nd edn, Longman, London, pp. 71–4

Skilbeck, M. (1976) 'School-based Curriculum Development and the Task of In-service Education', in E. Adams (ed.), *In-service Education and Teachers' Centres,* Pergamon Press, Oxford

Solihull Metropolitan Borough (1980) *Evaluating the Primary School,* Solihull

Southgate, V., Arnold, H. and Johnson, S. (1981) *Extending Beginning Reading,* Heinemann, London

Spooncer, F.A. (1964) *Group Reading Assessment,* Hodder & Stoughton,

London

Stansbury, D. (1979) 'Improving the Attitudes of School Leavers', *Forum*, 21, 3, pp. 97-8

Steadman, S. and Goldstein, H. (1982) 'Testing in Schools: The Teachers' View of Testing', Paper at the 1982 British Educational Research Association Annual Conference

Steinaker, N. and Bell, M.R. (1975) 'A proposed Taxonomy of Educational Objectives: The Experiential Domain', *Educational Technology*, 1, pp. 14-16

Stephens, J. (1977) 'Checkpoints in Primary Maths',*Contact*, 27, pp. 27-8

Stierer, B. (1982) 'Testing Teachers? A Critical Look at the Schools Council Project "Extending Beginning Reading" ', *Primary School Review*, 13, 1982

Stockport, Metropolitan Borough of (1982) *An Introduction to Self-Evaluation*, Stockport

Stubbs, M. and Delamont, S. (1976) *Explorations in Classroom Observation*, J. Wiley, London

Sumner, R. and Bradley, K. (1977) *Assessment for Transition*, NFER, Windsor

Thackray Reading-Readiness Profiles (1973) Hodder & Stoughton, Sevenoaks

Thompson, B., Schaub, P. and Mackay, D. (1968)*Manual to Accompany the Schools Council Initial Literacy Materials*, Longman Green, London

Thomson, M. (1979) 'The Aston Intervention Programme' in M. St J. Raggett (ed.), *Assessment and Testing of Reading*, Ward Lock, London, pp. 163-79

Thorndike, R.L. and Hagen, E. (1969) *Measurement and Evaluation in Psychology and Education*, J. Wiley, New York

Tomlinson, S. (1980) 'Ethnic Minority Parents and Education', in M. Craft, J. Raynor and L. Cohen (eds.), *Linking Home and School*, Harper & Row, London, pp. 186-99

Vincent, D. and Cresswell, M. (1976) *Reading Tests in the Classroom*, NFER, Windsor

Warnock Report (1978) *Report of the Warnock Committee of Enquiry into the Education of Handicapped Children and Young People*, HMSO, London

Whitfield, R. (1978) 'Choice within a National Framework for the School Curriculum', *Westminster Studies in Education*, 1, pp. 63-72

Wicksteed, D. and Hill, M. (1979) 'Is This You? — a Survey of Primary Teachers' Attitudes to Issues Raised in the Great Debate', *Education*

3-13, 7, 1, pp. 32-63

Wood, O. and Land, V. (1971) *Manual of Instructions, Verbal Test E.F.*, NFER, Windsor

Yardsticks (1975) *Criterion-referenced Tests in Mathematics*, Nelson, London

Young, D. (1968) *Group Reading Test*, Hodder & Stoughton, London

INDEX